SCOTTISH DOVECOTES

G. A. G. Peterkin

Drawings by
W. R. A. Logie

First published in
Coupar Angus, Scotland in 1980

List of Illustrations

I am grateful to the following for the use of illustrations, i.e. Figs. 8 & 12 – Ancient Monuments Commission, Department of the Environment; Fig. 16 – Miss Margaret Leven; Fig. 18 – the late Mr. John Gladstone; Fig. 21 – adapted from the paper by D. C. Bailey & M. C. Tindall. Fig. 26 – Commander R. M. Douglas, RN.

Contents

Acknowledgements

INTRODUCING this monograph, which is too brief to cover the subject completely, the author has a pleasant duty to perform; that is, to thank the people whose help has been greatly valued. First must come the late Dr A. Niven Robertson whose unremitting travels and research resulted in the production of a large volume on Scottish dovecotes, still, alas, in manuscript form. I was fortunate enough to 'inherit' his papers and photographs, including a copy of the charming work by A. O. Cooke, *A Book of Dovecotes* (1920).

The late Mr John Gladstone of Capenoch and the late Hon. Mrs I. G. Lindsay generously gave me all the information collected over the years by the former and by the latter's husband, the notable architect, the late Ian G. Lindsay. I gladly acknowledge the help given by Mr Stewart Cruden, Mr David Walker and Miss Kitty Cruft, all of the Inspectorate of the Ancient Monuments Commission for Scotland, and by Mr Trevor Royle.

Thanks are also due to Mr M. E. Taylor, County Planning Officer, Fife; to Miss Elizabeth Spittal, Depute Director of Planning, Renfrewshire; to Lady Maitland of Reswallie, near Forfar; to Dr J. Gordon Burgess, Forfar; to Commander R. M. Douglas, R. N. (Retd), Coppenhall; to Mrs Beaton, Hopeman; to Miss Margaret Leven, Kelso; and to Mr D. C. Bailey and Mrs Mary Tindall.

Although this work contains little reference to pigeon houses in England, I have derived much information from Mr Reginald Harrison, Shrewsbury, whose book on English dovecotes should soon be published, and from Captain P. N. Tatton Brown, R. N., of Wellow Manor House, near Bath.

Deep gratitude goes to the owners of dovecotes who have been so kind and helpful to an inquisitive visitor. To quote Michael Lewis, 'I have only to take out of their secret resting-place in my mind the many instances of real altruism which I have called from all sorts of ready helpers . . . all so equally eager to oblige; all so utterly innocent of self-aggrandisement and love of gain.'[1]

1. *Ancestors* (Hodder & Stoughton, 1966).

Origins

To some, especially townfolk, the pigeon is a dreary creature, as witness Anthony Carson: 'Pigeons, those dull, unmysterious city unemployables, dressed in their grey, second-hand suits'.[2] To others, like the late T. H. White, 'The pigeon . . . is a kind of quaker. She dresses in grey, a dutiful child, a constant lover, she knows like all philosophers that the hand of every man is against her'.[3]

As an old farmer said, 'Doocots are just a darned nuisance', and one must confess that nowadays they seldom have any useful purpose, though it is amazing what varied functions they can still serve, and there is a great fascination about them. Each is different, many are quaint, some are elegant and lovely. Frequently they are associated with historic or beautiful places, near castles and mansions, many of which are sadly decayed. The pastime of 'Spotting a Doocot' can add great interest to many a holiday, so that one not only has seen many charming doocots, but has visited some delightful parts of the country.

The origins of doocots are of great antiquity. At the prehistoric Skara Brae settlement in the Orkneys are holes suggestive of pigeon nests. The Middle East was the area where pigeon houses flourished – and still do. In 3000 B.C., during the fifth Egyptian dynasty, they were plentiful, and they still are in Egypt. To quote Lawrence Durrell, when he describes Nessim's country house, 'The main gateway was flanked to each side by a pigeon-house – those clumsy columns built of earthen pitchers pasted together anyhow with mud cement; which are characteristic of country houses in Egypt and which supplied the choicest dish for the country squire's table.'[4]

In Iran, dovecotes are usually in the form of large truncated cones of mud brick scattered in dozens over the fields, (Fig. 3), for there they use the pigeon dung as excellent manure for their fruit and vegetables, and do not eat the birds.

The Bible contains many references to pigeons from the time of Noah onwards; two quotations will suffice: 'Oh ye that dwell in Moab, leave the cities and dwell in the rock and be like the dove that maketh her nest in the side of the hole's mouth' (Jeremiah *48*, 28); 'Who are they that fly as a cloud

1

and as doves to their windows?' (Isaiah *60*, 8). The first shows that the doves were rock pigeons, precursors of the doves which later inhabited the cotes. In Scotland there are several caves containing pigeon holes for example, at Hawthornden Castle, Midlothian, and the Doo Cave, Fife.

According to Tavernier in his Persian travels Mildred Berkeley,[5] mentions that there were 10,000 pigeon houses in Ispahan alone and that every man, except a Christian, could build one on his own land. He adds: 'Some of the vulgar sort will turn Mohammedan to have that liberty.'

3. Iran dovecotes.

The Romans were enthusiastic pigeon-fanciers. Varro, who died in 23 B.C., mentions that doves were a considerable source of revenue and that in Rome and Florence the dovecotes were like monster beehives, holding 5,000 birds. Birds were fed for the table and high wages were paid to men who chewed white bread as special food for the young pigeons. Running water was provided so that the pigeons could drink and bathe.[6]

2

The Normans were responsible for introducing dovecotes to this country, perhaps from Italy or the Middle East. Sir John Glubb remarks: 'We are inclined nowadays to believe that before the invention of modern science, everything in the world moved with a slowness which to us would be unbearable. It is, therefore, of interest to know that Baybars, Sultan of Egypt, was able to receive messages from any part of the empire almost as rapidly as could be done by modern telegrams. Pigeons flew in relays, each flying only one stage. . . . Pigeons were more devoted to their mates than other birds. Only male pigeons were used to carry letters. The female was kept in the homing loft, when her husband was taken away to a staging post. As soon as he received his letter, his only idea was to join his wife. . . .'[7] As a result, letters could be sent from Damascus to Cairo in two to three days – a sad reflection on our present postal system. It is therefore not surprising that laboratory specimens are now being conveyed to a hospital at Plymouth by carrier pigeons.

The dovecotes introduced into Britain by the Normans were of the tun-bellied or beehive kind (Fig. 4). At first they were built only in the demesnes of the lords of the manor and at religious establishments, but later the wealthier burgesses were able to have cotes within the limits of their towns. The oldest one in Britain, once belonging to the Knights Hospitallers, is at Garway, Herefordshire, and has the inscription: 'In the year 1326, this dovecote was built by Brother Richard.'[8] It is possible that the oldest in Scotland is that at Crossraguel Abbey, Ayrshire. Niven Robertson quotes from the guide-book at Inchcolm: 'In the fifteen century stone vaults were inserted in the Abbey tower, to replace the timber floors, destroyed when Henry of Lancaster attacked the Abbey in 1384. When the

4. Waughton Castle.

5. Crossraguel Abbey.

vaults were inserted, the second floor was converted into a dovecote, nest holes being cut on all interior faces'. Crossraguel Abbey doocot probably dates from the sixteenth century (Fig. 5).

Although there are many of the beehive kind, the characteristic type in Scotland is the 'lean-to' or lectern (Fig. 2 & 6), well described by Robert Southey after his journey between Arbroath and Montrose in 1819: 'Two or three pigeon-houses in the fields of singular construction – slender but not narrow buildings, with a shelving roof in front, and a straight wall on the back from the summit of the roof – the whole being like the section of a house cut in half, from the ridge of the roof.'[9]

With the dissolution of the monasteries, pigeon cotes came into the possession of lords of the manor and lairds, and not infrequently one finds them built into castles: e.g. Hailes Castle (Fig. 7), Eastshield. Ministers of the Church of Scotland often had doocots near their churches, or in the kirk tower: e.g., Aberlady, Stenton (Fig. 8) Carrington and Torphichen Preceptory. Pigeons could be a mixed blessing; the beadle of Tyninghame Church 'got an allowance for pouther tae shoot the doos because they filet the seats' in the kirk.

6. Midhope Castle.

7. Hailes Castle.

Probably the oldest dated cote in Scotland is the fine one at Rochelhill in Angus, which bears the date 1565 (although it is possible that the tablet was taken from an older building) and the motto 'Hop in the Hiest'. The huge and lovely one at Mertoun (Cover I) is dated 1576, and those at Athelstaneford and Tranent (both near churches and of the lean-to type) are of the late sixteenth century.

The Romans called dovecotes by the names columbarium, peristeron and peristerotrophion,[10] and monks used the word columbarium in Britain as elsewhere. In England, the Old English word for pigeon was culver, so the birds' homes were known as culverhouses, although more often they were called pigeon-houses or dovecotes. In Essex people used the word duffus, while in Scotland we usually term them doocots, sometimes spelled 'ducat' or 'dowcat'. This is reminiscent of the Norse and Danish due.[11] In Holland the structure is known as a duivetil or duivekot.

2. *On to Timbuctoo*
3. *The Sword in the Stone* (Collins, 1966)
4. *Balthazar* (Faber & Faber, 1958).
5. Article on dovecotes in *The Home Counties Magazine* (Vol. VIII, 1906).
6. *A Book of Dovecotes* (T. N. Foulis, 1920).
7. *Soldiers of Fortune: The Story of the Mamelukes* (Hodder & Stoughton, 1973).
8. Cooke, ibid.
9. *Journal of a Tour in Scotland* (John Murray, 1929 edition).
10. Cooke, ibid.
11. *Pigeon Cotes and Dovehouses of Essex* (Simpkin Marshall, 1931).

Uses

Of course the main reason for keeping pigeons was to provide food for wealthier people all the year round, but especially in the winter months, when poor people often starved. The introduction of turnips from Sweden in the eighteenth century provided winter food for humans as well as cattle, and so fewer and fewer doocots were erected. Sir Arthur Bryant says: 'An equally resented monopoly was the lord's dovecote and "free warren" from which hordes of pigeons and rabbits descended on the peasant's crops.'[12]

In a letter to A. O. Cooke, Mrs Edith Bourne quotes from Professor Plummer's book *Food and Health* in which he says: 'The people did not thrive upon their salted and dried rations and there was much scurvy in the Middle Ages, especially in London so it was sometimes called "The London Disease". The Nobility and Lords of the Manor had their dovecotes and game preserves to provide themselves with animal food during the winter.'

Young pigeons (squabs) were esteemed a delicacy throughout the year and we note that in Essex, F. G. Emmison writes: 'Pigeons from the (Ingatestone) Hall dovecote were eaten regularly from April to September. The heaviest drawing in 1552 took place in August. 'Pigeons taken out of the dovehouse this week three score pair.' The total drawn between Easter and Michaelmas was 1,080, no mean source of food . . . pigeon pie, therefore, frequently appeared in those months.'[13] Of course, in Scotland, pigeons were mainly eaten in winter-time.

The birds were served in different ways (one can still find the recipes in many cookery books, but, alas, not in Marian McNeill's excellent book *Scots Kitchen*,) e.g., as pie, roasted, stewed (sometimes with mushrooms or raisins), cold, or as a salmi. Marion Thorne Roberts remarks: 'Many were the treasured recipes for the cooking and dressing of squabs. One former housewife, whose favourite method has been handed down to us, recommends that squabs be eaten when ten days old, and preferably in the month of January, when, in her opinion, "they be best for the stomach and to yield, among the curious in eating, about two shillings or eighteenpence

7

apiece". She advises that they be broiled over a gentle fire and that, as they possess no gall-bladder, the liver should be left inside, salt, pepper and butter placed inside the body and the bird sewn up with a packthread.[14] She also mentions the recipe which divulges the secret method of one 'monsieur la Fontaine, an excellent cook in Paris – that a most succulent stew is made out of runts with mushrooms and shallots'.

Dove's dung was used in Scotland to some extent, but was a valuable export in France, and in the Middle East is still as important as ever as a fertiliser. John Gladstone quotes from the General Report on the Agriculture . . . of Scotland, 1814: 'Though there are many dovecotes in Scotland and although the dung is in general carefully collected, yet, on the whole, the quantity is inconsiderable. In former times the pigeons' dung was reduced to a fine powder, by the operation of threshing with flails. . . . Pigeons' dung is more generally bestowed on wheat or barley than on any other crop. . . .'[15] The dung was also used in tanning, for the removal of hair from the pelt.

The owners of castles needed their doocots not only for a source of food, but also for the making of gunpowder and Charles I in 1625 ordained that owners of pigeon houses might not pave them with stone or brick but were to use nothing but good sound earth. Eric Parker tells us that 'in the year 1560 a German captain Gerrard Honrick agreed, for the sum of Three Hundred Pounds, to instruct Englishmen "in the trew and perfect art of making salt peter". The art consisted in mixing the excrement of animals, "the blacker the better" and one of the chief sources was the soil of pigeon houses'.[16] The dung's rich content of potassium nitrate (the villainous salt peter mentioned by Shakespeare) was mixed with black earth and sulphur to form gunpowder.

In medicine in the old days the pigeon was used in many ways, and was often applied to the feet or breast in cases of serious illness. Several famous authors such as John Donne, John Evelyn, Samuel Pepys and Jeremy Taylor refer to these 'last of remedyes'. James Primrose says: 'It is a usual thing with them in Mons peliers, to apply young pigeons, cloven through the middle . . . to the region of the heart, to comfort the heart.'[17] Francis Willughby recommends the following: 'A live pigeon cut asunder along the backbone and clapt upon the

8

head mitigates fierce humours and discusses melancholy sadness. Hence it is most proper medicine in the plurisie, headache, melancholy and gout.'[18] Dr Salmon gives the following prescription (which I must confess I have never prescribed): 'Of the powder of the dung of pigeons, beaten and sifted 2 ozs; of Bear's Grease 4 ozs; Pepper in powder 1 oz; oil of Cummin ½ oz.; mix for an ointment against baldness.'[19]

At one time it was firmly believed that no one would die if pigeon feathers were used in pillows. James Grant, referring to the mother in *Philip Rollo*, wrote: 'But she died and on a bed of pigeon feathers too, to the dismay of all the wise women in Cromarty.'

12. *The Fire and the Rose* (Collins, 1965).
13. *Tudor Secretary* (Longmans, Green, 1961).
14. 'Dovecots by the Way'; *S.M.T. Magazine* (1940).
15. *Personal Communication*.
16. *Surrey* (Robert Hale).
17. *De Vulgi Erroris in Medicina* (1638).
18. *Ornithologia* (1678).
19. *Seplasium or English Physician*.

Legal Aspects

In Scotland, as in England, the laws concerning dovecotes were numerous and favoured the wealthier people. John Gladstone has extracted the following from the General Index to the Acts of Parliament of Scotland: 'destroyers of dovecotes to be punished' (1424); 'breaking of doocots to be a point of dittay, the unlaw to be ten pounds, with amends for the damage; parents of children committing the offence to be fined 13s 4d or to give up the children to the judge "to be leschit, scurgit and doung according to the falt" ' (1503); 'breakers of dovecotes to be punished as thieves; the act extended to those giving assistance to the misdoers' (1535); 'shooting doves with gun or bow forbidden under pain or forfeiture of moveables, or for the first fault forty days' imprisonment, for the second, loss of the right hand' (1567); 'justices of peace ordained to put the Acts of Parliament in execution against breakers of "Dow houses"; the punishment to be a "pecunial sum" ' (1617, 1655, 1661); 'no person to build a dovecot who is not possessed of 10 chalders' victual rent within two miles thereof (1 chalder equalled 16 bolls of 1¼ hundredweight); one dovecot only to be built within the said bounds (1617).'[20] Robert Douglas[21], father of Commander R. M. Douglas, who also is an expert on doocots, has given an excellent description of the action brought in 1751 by the Lord Lyon, Alexander Brodie of Brodie, against the wicked Sir Robert Gordon of Gordonstoun, where under these laws the case was settled in favour of the latter. Douglas also states that a dovecote breaker and thief might suffer capital punishment on a third offence, and also mentions an Act of 1503 which 'Ordains ilk lord and laird to make them dowecots', and a Statute of 1597 by which the offender might be put in the stocks for forty-eight hours. There were also several Acts which forbade anyone to take 'foulis' out of the dovecotes without licence of the owner. Niven Robertson records from a book by Laurence Melville that a learned judge startled an entrant to the Faculty of Advocates by asking, 'Wha may hae doos?'

Despite the harsh laws, many tough Scots broke them often, and numerous examples could be quoted. For instance, in 1621, 'in contravention of the laws against wearing hagbuts,

10

Allan Deans, callit "the millair", in Hawick, Robert Armstrong, smith there, callit "the cunning craftsman", Robert Scott, merchant called "Geordie's Hobie", have from January to November worn hagbuts and pistolets, hes schot and slayne great numbers of their neighbours' proper dowis, and use the same for revenge upon all persons against whom they bear quarrel.' In 1653, Colin Campbell, owner of a doocot on Glasgow Green, complained to the magistrates of the boys troubling his dows 'by chapping on the door of his dowcat'. Today, however, boys appear to be much more destructive, for in The Sunday Post we read that Mr Shannon at Easterhouse, Glasgow, 'has had his loft hit by vandals more times than he cares to remember. His stock has been wiped out time and again'. Tatton Brown quotes from The Sportsman's Dictionary of 1725, where the builder is told to 'plant the pigeon house in the middle of a courtyard and near enough to the house that the master of the family may keep in awe those who go in or come out.'[22]

20. Gladstone, ibid.
21. *The Dovecotes of Moray* (Courant & Courier Office, 1931).
22. *Personal Communication*.

Literary References

A long essay could be written about this subject. Many will recall, in Stendhal's The Scarlet and The Black, the signal made from her tall dovecote by the Mayor's wife, Mme de Rénal, to her lover Julien Sorel. In Swann's Way, Marcel Proust says: 'She would have preferred to take a house that had a Gothic dovecote or some other piece of antiquity, as would have a pleasant effect on the mind.' In the same way, Soames Forsyte, in The Silver Spoon, was soothed by looking at his old dovecote. A tun-bellied large cote appears in A. E. W. Mason's Fire over England and a pigeon loft in John Masefield's Jim Davis, while, in Romeo and Juliet, the old nurse was 'sitting in the sun under the dovehouse wall'.

11

Osbert Sitwell, in Tales my Father Taught Me, remarks: 'At one place we visited the house had just been pulled down and there only remained a square red pigeon cote, like a truncated tower which still bore the arms of a Sacheverell – a building, no doubt, with an economic purpose.' And in Evelyn Waugh's The Loved One, there is the fantastic cemetery with its dovecote. In The Bible in Spain, George Borrow talks about the priest who invited him to see his pigeon house and who told him that he permitted no other cote in his village.

Also set in Spain is Neil Paterson's short story 'And Delilah', about the peasant's pigeon loft and his pigeon The Black Devil. Many other Scots authors could be mentioned, including Sir Walter Scott, who describes so well in Waverley the doocot at Tullyveolan; John Buchan in Witch Wood refers to the old dovecote at Calidon. When young, one was thrilled by the events concerning the doocot in The New Road by Neil Munro and in The Interloper by Violet Jacob, who also wrote the pleasant poem entitled 'The doocot up the braes', although there seems to have been no pigeon cote at her old home, the House of Dun. Baroness Nairne showed some interest in them, as witness the poems 'The Twa Doos' and 'The Fife Laird' in which she writes: 'The Laird is hame wi' a' his ain

> Below the Lomond hill
> Right glad to see his sheep again,
> His dookit and his mill'.

Dr Alexander Pennycuik penned a satire on a neighbour because 'Thou didst a base absurd and scurvy deed to shoot my doves upon the dovecote heid', at Romanno.

Structure and Design

Practically all Scottish dovecotes are built of local stone, usually with rubble in the case of the beehive type, and with rubble and ashlar in the other types. Sometimes we come across beautiful examples of mason work, as in the red sandstone of the Thornton cote.

The *Beehive* has an opening at the top (Fig. 9 and 10), sometimes surmounted by a lantern or louvre. Most of these were built many years ago and not later than the seventeenth century, and the thicker the walls the older the building. Some are quite small but others are impressive in size like those at Mertoun and Monteviot.

In the Lothians, there are a number of fine beehives, such as those at Dirleton Castle, Drylawhill (Fig. 11), Northfield, Nunraw Abbey (Fig. 12), Corstorphine and Lochend. Other notable ones are at Bogward, St Andrews, Fetteresso Castle and Gordonstoun.

The *Rectangular* and *Square* types usually have lean-to roofs, commonly slated, but they may be covered by pantiles or stone slabs. Sometimes, especially in the older examples, those with a ridge roof are covered with large stone slabs, e.g., Pittendreich, Morayshire.

The *Cylinder* pattern is relatively common and some are extremely attractive. Worth mentioning are those at Lessuden, St Boswells (well known to Sir Walter Scott in his youth); Lady Kitty's Garden, Haddington, once used as a dwelling (Fig. 13); Elvingston, near Haddington; Whitburgh; Leuchars Castle, Fife; Fothringham, Angus; and Boath (Fig. 14), situated on the mound from which Montrose directed the Battle of Auldearn. At Carlunan, Inveraray, is the tall white cote built in 1747 for the famous third Duke of Argyll, who paid £48 to the mason who carried out the plans to the satisfaction of the Duke, the architect and William Adam. There is a fireplace on the ground floor, so it may have been used as a summer-house with a pleasing prospect.

Of the Pentagonal, Hexagonal and Octagonal varieties, a solitary pentagonal one exists in Scotland, at Nisbet House, Berwickshire; octagonal ones are the commonest and include Wallhouse, fast becoming a ruin, Murdostoun Castle, Bow-

9. Monteviot House.

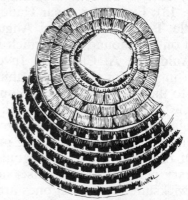

10. Monteviot House – interior

14

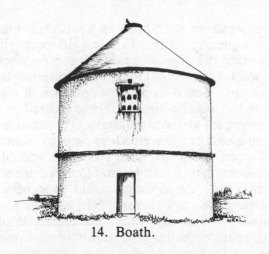

14. Boath.

butts, West Pitkierie, Durie, and Craigiebuckler. Those with hexagonal sides are fewer although beautiful, e.g. Redhall, Edinburgh, with its coat-of-arms and potence; Grange Hall, Morayshire and Megginch Castle, Perthshire (Fig. 16), with its six pointed arches and a ship as a weathervane. This ship, according to Mrs. Cherry Drummond of Megginch, is a model of the "General Elliot", on which Captain Robert Drummond sailed as Captain in 1783.

Doors are low and narrow, about 5 feet high, to prevent the egress of the birds, were sometimes made of iron, and sometimes they were double as at Waterybutts. Most two-chambered cotes have two doors, but there are some with only one outer door and an inner door connecting the two chambers.

Stringcourses are a good indication that a building is, or has been, a doocot, and there may be even two or three of them. These projecting ridges were made smooth and slippery, so that predators such as rats could not gain a foothold. Instances are known in England of iron spikes being set vertically below the stringcourse, so as to impale the rats when they fell attempting to surmount it.

Entrance holes for the birds differed greatly. As noted above, pigeons entered the beehive type by a louvre, and this was sometimes the case in cotes with a conical or pyramidal roof. In the rectangular and square types, arched holes were provided just below the roof, or horizontally along the roof,

15

and dormer windows with holes in a wooden board or in the stone are frequently found. In some doocots, shutters were provided so that the pigeons could not escape when the owner required food for his table. Donald A. Smith refers to 'wooden flaps with a pulley cord to prevent entrance at night',[23] found in some English pigeon-houses. These existed in a few Scots ones, for example, at Johnstounburn, Thornton and at Blackwood, Dumfriesshire, described so well by John Gladstone: 'It has an opening of six inches outside and fifteen inches inside. A shutter which can be manipulated from below by a string is attached; the opening could thus be closed when pigeon-catching was in progress.'[24] In a letter to John Gladstone, dated 7th January 1927, Mr James Waugh, joiner, Auldgirth, writes regarding the repair of this doocot: 'There used to be a patent trap door which no doubt was intended to protect the pigeons from thieves'. Possibly these flaps served both functions. Rarely one finds iron spikes or hoops which may have been intended to protect the birds from hawks, or iron plates set at a steep angle to stop the invasion of rats. Sometimes we find a few entrance holes in gables, but as a rule the roof faced south and landing ledges were provided for the pigeons to sit in the sun, protected from the wind.

17. Glamis Castle.

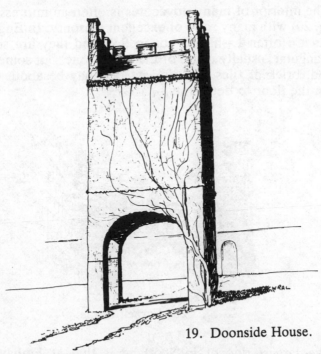

19. Doonside House.

Crowsteps are often found, as on many other Scots building, sometimes widely spaced, and sometimes on the back wall, as at Glamis Castle (Fig. 17) and Hospitalfield. Finials, mainly in the form of stone balls, are set into the back wall or the gables, as at Alderstone, Cleish, Hermitage of Braid, Preston Tower (Fig. 18) and West Pitkierie. Weathervanes are more frequently seen topping louvred doocots, but are occasionally observed on the rear wall of lean-to cotes. Weathercocks, and vanes in the shape of fish, a ship and so on may add to the attractiveness of these buildings. Windows, apart from dormer ones, can be square or rectangular, but typical are the small round or oval windows, with an iron grill above the doors, or on gables. On two or three doocots, such as that at Drylaw, are vertical sundials on skewputs (cornerstones) on which, particularly in Angus, are occasionally carved as human faces. Tablets with coats-of-arms, the date of construction, and the initials of the owner may be found, e.g. at Meldrum House. Battlements are seen mainly in the tower type of the early nineteenth century (Fig. 19).

17

The interior of many dovecotes is often an impressive sight (Fig. 20) with many rows of excellent masonry. In England the nests are often L-shaped but in Scotland they are square or rectangular, usually made of the local stone, but sometimes of wood, brick or tiles. The lowest tier may be about two feet from the floor to deter rats.

20. Farnell Castle.

The largest doocot in Scotland is that at Finhaven, and according to Niven Robertson, it had 2,421 nestholes, compared with Newliston which had 2,604, Kinnimonth 2,364, Johnstounburn 2,140, Nether Liberton 2,072, Midhope 2,006 and Hermitage of Braid 1,965. It is worth noting that five of these seven are in the Lothians.

Thanks to the excellent work of the Angus Historical Society, the Finhaven doocot has been completely renovated. The west chamber is now a doocot museum, while the east one is still a pigeon house.

In the days of ancient Rome, columbaria were sometimes provided with running water for bathing and drinking purposes. The only evidence of such concern for the 'doos' in Scotland is a small stone bath, once in the Ravelston cote.

I have neither seen nor heard of any English dovecote of the lectern or lean-to type, although those with ridge roofs are not uncommon. For example, in Worcestershire, eleven of the latter have been noted. The typical English cote is the tunbellied or cylindrical one, but various others are found such as

8 Stenton Tower –
churchyard tower with entrance holes

11 Drylawhill, East Lothian

*12 Nunraw Abbey, East Lothian –
old beehive with later additions such as louvre*

*13 Lady Kitty's Garden, East Lothian –
once used as a cottage*

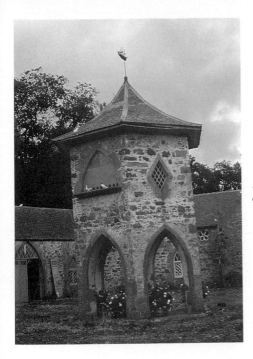

*16 Megginch Castle, Perthshire –
attractive and unusual*

*26 Gordonstoun, Morayshire –
windmill converted to a doocot*

22 Saltoun Home Farm, East Lothian – good example of farmyard type

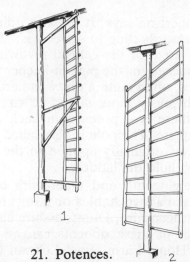

21. Potences.

half-timbered square or octagonal. For the large tunbellied and cylindrical ones, stone is most often the building material, but by far the commonest substance is brick. A few Scots ones were made of brick e.g. Brickswold, Midlothian; Dubton and Powis Mains in Angus.

France possesses a vast number of pigeon-houses, especially in the Dordogne and Tarn regions. Farther north, huge circular cotes are found, sometimes decorated with red, purple, yellow and green bricks, while polished bricks may take the place of stringcourses, as do tiles in Languedoc. In the south of France, because of the 'mistral' wind, square buildings with lean-to roofs have evolved, often with hoods or towers to protect the birds. On these one often finds ceramic finials of pleasing appearance. From these derive the Scots lecterns.

Many French dovecotes were destroyed during the Revolution, for only three classes of landed proprietor were permitted to build them i.e. 'grand justiciars'; 'seigneurs de fief'; and 'seigneurs de censive', although ordinary folk were allowed to have 'fuies'. 'Colombiers à pied' were those planted solidly on the ground, and 'colombiers sur piliers' were those which were arcaded (as in Fig. 19), on pillars, posts or on stone 'mushrooms' which acted as stringcourses.

During the nineteenth century, the old restrictions having vanished, many new dovecotes arose and often were included in farm buildings, as in this country.

As Niven Robertson says 'It is extraordinary how the old French Norman words cling to dovecotes.' The word potence (Fig. 21) is still used for the central revolving poles to which ladders were attached for the pigeon-keeper to climb up to the higher nest holes, often quite a dizzy and arduous ascent. The potence was obviously more suited to circular cotes but at Pinkie House there is a potence in each chamber and the chambers are square. The pole is also called the arbre and the word potence was originally applied to the gallows or transverse bars which hold the ladders.

In the late eighteenth and nineteenth centuries, pigeons were often housed above stables or farmyard buildings, especially so in Aberdeenshire, Dumfriesshire and Ross-shire. Excellent examples of these doocots can be seen at Harelaw Farm, Saltoun Home Farm, East Lothian (Fig. 22) and Arbuthnott Mains, Kincardineshire which has no less than seventy-two entrance holes.

The old French term fuie was originally applied to a wooden box hung on the gable of a house or outbuilding, and this name is now applied to the small dovecotes in the gable-ends of a house

Twin cotes are uncommon, but occur at Ackergill, Caithness; Balcaskie, Fife; Balmakewan, Kincardineshire; Culter House and Newmains of Tolquhoun, Aberdeenshire.

15. Auchmacoy.

20

In Scotland, there are many dovecotes which might be termed eccentric. At Pitmuies, Angus, there is one dated 1643 which has small circular towers at both ends of the front wall, each lighted by glazed cruciform windows. The western tower is part of the doocot, but the other has no connection with it. Also in Angus, the Careston doocot is surrounded by a moat, possibly to deter cats and rats, and that at Edzell Castle Mains has a ridge roof of stone slabs and a curious corbelled turret. The small one at Banchory, only seven feet square, has a pink granite foundation and the upper part is built of wooden slats. The finest doocot in Aberdeenshire is at Auchmacoy (Fig. 15). The lower part is tunbellied and on top is a rectangular building with a ridge roof and crowstepped gables. Human faces are carved on the skewputs. The one at Castle Huntly, Perthshire, is square and once had projecting round turrets at each corner.

At each angle of what was once the walled garden of Amisfield House, near Haddington (Fig. 23) are four small buildings like Greek temples with Ionic pillars and domed roofs; the one at the south-east is a dovecote with an entrance in the roof.

The three cotes at Huntington, Lundin and Edmonstone have the appearance of small chapels (Fig. 24) – perhaps Scotland is the only country in which such dovecotes are to be found. At Phantassie, East Lothian (Fig. 25) under the aegis of the National Trust, is the well-known beehive doocot with a hood shaped like a horse-shoe; it was once a windmill.

I. L. Donnachie and N. K. Stewart, in a paper on Scottish windmills, state that 'disused windmills were often converted to other uses. Many survived as dovecotes, ice-houses and look-out towers.'[25] Those mentioned are Monkton, Bielside, Balgone Barns, Melville House, Gordonstoun (Fig. 26), Phantassie (Fig. 25), Crail, and Gunsgreen. Others probably in this category are Dumbarrow, Sauchie and Millhill, Gartley.

Below the lovely octagonal cote at Murdostoun Castle, Lanarkshire, is an ice-house in an excellent state of preservation.

When dovecotes are in an upper chamber, the lower floor is often used for a variety of purposes, e.g. henhouse, storeroom etc. It is after they are abandoned that these buildings assume a completely different role. For example, several old

21

24. Edmonstone.

cotes have become cottages, usually quite charming, such as Hilltown of Knapp in the Carse of Gowrie; Castlewigg; Ravelston (Figs. 27 and 28); Humbie, East Lothian; Blackwood, Lanarkshire; another large one, that at Newliston, is converted into a cottage. The pleasant doocot at Huntington sometimes serves as a horse-box, and at Lour in Angus, one of the two doors has been enlarged so that the doocot can be used as a cart shed. Other doocots have been used as a wine-cellar, a granary, gun-powder stores, a pumping station, and at Eskhill House the building has been made into a studio.

Doocots can be found on several golf courses including Banchory, Cambuslang, Capelrig, Cawder, Kirroughtree and

Ratho Park, and Commander R. M. Douglas gave me a photograph of a single-chambered rectangular one at Old Troon, of which there now seems to be no trace. It is pleasant to record that as a rule the golf clubs which own these keep them in excellent repair.

It is distressing that so many doocots have vanished completely, and many are in such a ruinous state that they will soon disappear. However, with the help of the Ancient Monuments Commission for Scotland (Department of the Environment), there is a good prospect that a few notable ones will be restored each year and those already in their care will be maintained. The Scottish National Trust, sorely handicapped for lack of funds, keeps those under its charge in admirable order.

One should not forget the pigeon houses kept in excellent condition, thanks to people such as the Planning Officers of Regional Councils, and to owners who love their doocots and despite rising building costs have kept them in reasonable repair.

25. Phantassie.

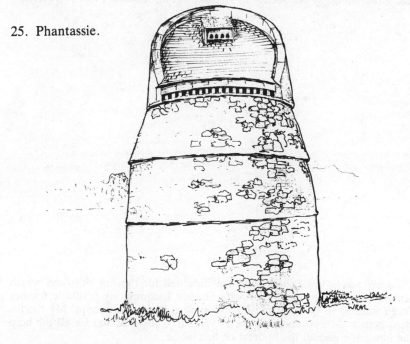

The following list of edifices is bound to be inaccurate in many respects; some may have vanished and some may have been omitted. The author would be grateful for any information which would repair any deficiencies. It will be observed that in the following list I have not given clear directions as to the locations of doocots, e.g. no map references, although I myself have noted these. This was done so as not to deprive readers of the pleasure of discovering for themselves doocots so often hidden and remote.

It is important for those visiting dovecotes to keep in mind that many of these buildings are situated on private property, so that permission to visit them should be sought.

Once only has the author met with a cold reception. It was later discovered that this man was about to destroy the house and dovecote, as he was a property dealer.

23. *Pigeon Cotes and Dovehouses of Essex* (Simpkin Marshall, 1931)
24. *The Dovecote at Blackwood*, Transactions of the Dumfries and Galloway Historical and Antiquarian Society (1929).
25. *Proceedings of the Society of Antiquaries of Scotland* (Vol. XCVIII).

"To my son-in-law Bill Logie I am indebted for the line drawings which enhance this work, and to my wife Sheena I express my gratitude for her keen interest in doocots and for her typing of the manuscript. My thanks also goes to Mr. Robert Benzies of William Culross & Son for all the help he has given and all the interest he has taken.

Bibliography

1. Astruc, Henri; 'Les Pigeonniers Tarnais'; Imprimerie Cooperative du Sud-oest; Albi, Tarn, France; N.D.
2. Beaton, Elizabeth; 'The Doocots of Moray'; Moray Field Club; 1978.
3. Cooke, A. O.; 'A Book of Dovecotes'; T. N. Foulis; 1920.
4. Bailey, D. C. and Tindall, M. C.; 'Dovecotes of East Lothian'; Trans. Anc. Mon. Soc., II, 1963.
5. Douglas, Robert; 'The Dovecotes of Moray'; Courant and Courier Office, Elgin; 1931.
6. Peters, W. D.; 'Dovecotes and Pigeon Lofts in Herefordshire'; Hereford and Worcester County Council; 1979.
7. Pridham, J. C.; 'Dovecotes and Pigeon Cotes in Worcestershire'; Hereford and Worcester County Council; 1974.
8. Robertson, A. Niven; unpublished illustrated manuscript (copy in the Library of the Society of Antiquaries of Scotland). A wonderful book full of information and the fruits of many years of research.
9. Smith, Donald; 'Pigeon Cotes and Dovehouses of Essex'; Simpkin Marshall; 1931.
10. Williamson, Henry; 'The Scandaroon'; Macdonald; 1972.

Geographical Order of Listed Dovecotes

A. *Borders* – Wigtownshire, Kirkcudbrightshire, Dumfriesshire, Roxburghshire, Selkirkshire, Peeblesshire and Berwickshire.
B. *Lothians* – East Lothian, Midlothian, Edinburgh and West Lothian.
C. *West Country* – Lanarkshire, Ayrshire, Renfrewshire, Glasgow and Dumbartonshire.
D. *Clackmannan, Kinross and Fife*.
E. *Stirlingshire and Perthshire*.
F. *Angus and Kincardineshire*.
G. *Aberdeenshire and Banffshire*.

H. *Morayshire, Nairn and Inverness-shire.*
I. *Ross-shire, Sutherland and Caithness.*
J. *Argyll and The Islands* – Bute, Argyll, the Hebrides, the
    Orkneys and the Shetlands

It will be noted that dovecotes have been classified by counties rather than by Regions, which still appear to be unpopular.

List of Scottish Dovecotes

Explanation of Symbols (Modified from 'Dovecotes of East Lothian' by D. C. Bailey and M. C. Tindall, Transactions of the Ancient Monuments Society Vol. II, 1963).

*	– worth a visit
⊙	– beehive type
●	– cylindrical
■	– square
▬	– rectangular
⊏⊐	– two-chambered rectangular
▲	– pentagonal, hexagonal, octagonal or eccentric
F	– in farm or stable offices
T	– in towers
Blank	– author's ignorance
D. of E.	– Department of the Environment
N.T.S.	– National Trust, Scotland

18 Preston Tower, East Lothian – elegant lectern with finials

23 Amisfield, East Lothian – like a Greek temple, with entrance on roof

27 Ravelston House, Edinburgh – double lectern, with unusual entrance holes

28 Ravelston House – converted into a cottage

WIGTONSHIRE

Barrwhanny Farm, Kirkinner. Late 18th century. Beaded doorway.

Castlewigg, near Whithorn. F. Now part of a cottage and has chimneys.

Corsewall House, Kirkcolm. T. Round tower.

Culreoch, Isle of Whithorn. ■ 16th century. Whitewashed with three stringcourses; ridge roof.

Genoch House. ● With three courses of red brick under eaves; slated ogee roof and small lantern with five openings.

Glasserton House Farm, near Whithorn. F. Two-storey square; dormer window and, below, V-opening with holes.

Lochryan House, Old Luce. ● Early 18th century. Two storey.

Myrton Castle, near Monreith.

Physgill House, Whithorn. F. In farm steading; whitewashed with lantern and chimneys.

Portpatrick. ● Ancient? In churchyard, poor preservation.

Tonderghie steading, Whithorn. F. Over archway.

KIRKCUDBRIGHTSHIRE

Arbigland, near Kirkbean. F. 18th century. Over stable archway.

Barcaple Stable Archways, Tongland. F. 18th century. Lean-to.

Brickwoods, Queen Street, Castle Douglas. F. In gable.

Carleton Stables, Borgue. F. 1833.

Chipperkyle, Kirkpatrick Durham. ■

Corbieton House, Haugh of Urr. ■ Four-sided pyramidal roof.

Cumstoun, Twynholm.

Gategill. F. Stables.

Greenlaw, Crossmichael. ■ Ruinous.

Gribdae Stables near Kirkcudbright. F. In gable.

Kelton Mains, near Castle Douglas. F.

Kirkhouse, Kirkgunzeon. 18th century.

Kirroughtree House, Newton Stewart.* ▲ Octagonal, white-washed, with pyramidal slated roof. Also small cote in roof of stables.

St Mary's Isle, Kirkcudbright

Walton Park, at stables tower. F. Early 19th century.

DUMFRIESSHIRE

Annan, 18 Scott Street.

Annan, Queensberry Arms. ■ 18th century.

Blackwood * near Closeburn. F. Stables, square, white-washed, pyramidal slate roof. (For details see 'The Dovecote at Blackwood' by John Gladstone, Transactions of the Dumfries and Galloway Natural History and Antiquaries Society (11th Jan. 1929)).

Broats, Kirkpatrick Fleming. F. In gable of outbuilding.

Castlemilk, near Lockerbie. F. In tower.

Closeburn Castle. F. 18th century. In stables.

Cowdens St Mungo. F. In loft.

Dalswinton, Kirkmahoe. ● 18th century.

Denbie, Dalton. ▲ 18th century. Octagonal, slated roof with weathervane; in excellent repair.

Fairy Knowe, Kirkpatrick Fleming. F. In stable block.

Faulding Cleuch, Kirkpatrick Fleming. F. In barn.

Friar's Carse, near Dumfries. F. In steading.

Glenae House, near Dumfries. F. In garden building, top of three storeys; brick walls with coigns of red sandstone; entrance in east wall; slated conical roof.

Greencroft, Annan.

Gribton House. F. Dated 1810. Rectangular tower above farmcourt pend; venetian window on east side below cote.

Hitehill, Cummertrees. F. In farm building.

Kemyss Hall, Kirkmahoe. 1775.

Kirkland, Kirkmichael. F. Part of steading.

Kirkmahoe. Late 17th or early 18th century.

Kirkwood, Dalton. F. Part of stables.

Lann Hall, Tynron. F. Whitewashed with dormer above rectangular high door.

Marchfield Farm, near Dumfries. F. Entrance high in west wall; in each wall one stringcourse with entrance holes over it.

Milnhead, Kirkmahoe. 17th to 18th century.

Netherwood, south of Dumfries. F. Stables.

Orchard, Hoddam, nr. Ecclefechan. F. Loft in steading.

Uppermoor, Cummertrees. F. In gable of farm.

Woodhouselees. F. In steading.

Wyseby, Kirkpatrick Fleming. ▲ Octagonal.

ROXBURGHSHIRE

Cavers Carre House. ⊞ Probably early 18th century despite plaque over entrance dated 1532? With one door only.

Darnick Tower. T. Ridge-roofed watch chamber with vaulted roof; one entrance hole with landing ledge.

Edgerston House. ▲ Octagonal with round window on south wall; roof conical and slated; south dormer window has arched opening.

Grahamslaw. ⊙ Entrance facing west; round opening in roof.

Knowesouth House, * near Jedburgh. ⊞ With crowstepped gables; doors on south side; lean-to slated roof with two dormer windows; partly boarded, still used by pigeons.

Lessuden House, * St Boswells. ● Slated roof with small slated louvre on four wooden pillars. In good condition.

Melrose Abbey *. ▬ With entrance on north side to stable; slated roof with high dormer window and two skylights; crowsteps on west gable. (D. of E.)

Monteviot House. * ⊙ Large battlemented tun-bellied with over 1,000 nests. Entrance holes on south side; corbelled roof with large stones at opening and louvre consisting of two huge flagstones on four legs; above this four carved stone legs supporting a stone ball finial. (Fig. 9 and 10)

Pinnacle Farm. * ■ 18th century. With oval window above south east entrance and entrance holes above window; roofless.

Sunlaws Mill. F. On farm buildings.

Also at Sunlaws, Dove Cave with nest holes.

Niven Robertson gives a list of fifteen vanished cotes in Roxburghshire.

SELKIRKSHIRE

Broadmeadows. ▬ Central dormer window with twelve holes; slate roof with skylight; faces south.

Carterhaugh. ■ Ruined lean-to roof; eight entrance holes in long dormer, well up on roof.

The Haining. ▬ Ruinous with entrance in front wall; window in west gable.

29

PEEBLESSHIRE

Broughton Place. ● Modern turreted conical roof; doocot in top storey. Weathervane of man chasing pigeon.

Cardrona House. ■■ Seven crowsteps with a skewput on each gable; window on west gable; slated roof above rear wall disintegrating.

Cringletie House. ■ With four entrance holes in south wall; conical slated roof.

Garvald, near West Linton. F. 'In the end gable of a byre is a pigeon-loft of unusual design.'

Halmyre House. ■ In upper half of building

Kailzie House. ■■ Dated 1698. On back wall three ball finials; crowstepped gables with skewput. In good order.

Macbiehill House. ● Ruined; foundations only remain.

Noblehouse Farm. F. Dated 1829. End gable of the mill is a pigeon loft.

Polmood, Drumelzier. ■■ Slated roof; 2 dormer windows. Right one blocked up, crowsteps, slated roof in good shape. Turbine in lower part.

Romanno House ● Completely ruined.

The Whim. ● 'Decapitated' and used as a store.

Niven Robertson gives a list of six vanished cotes in Peebleshire.

BERWICKSHIRE

Ayton Castle ☉ Over the entrance, tablet with date 1743 and initials T R & E W; near outhouses; with octagonal louvre and ball finial.

Cherrytrees, near Yetholm. F. In Farm offices.

Coldstream. Nos. 1, 2 & 3 Dovecot Cottages – no sign of entrance holes.

Corsbie, Legerwood. ■ became unsafe, removed about 1973.

Dryburgh House.* ● On lintel date insertion D 1828 E, for David Erskine. Roof round and slated; no doveholes; now a pumping house.

Edrington House. ■■ According to Miss Margaret Leven, it has now vanished.

Gunsgreen. T. Round tower in farm steading; a converted

windmill; well in basement; roof timber and tiles; string-course gone.

Hirsel, Coldstream. F. square tower in stable offices.

Longformacus House. ● Slated ogee roof; slated louvre has pole with two metal balls, compass pointers and metal arrow.

Manderston House. ■ Modern with slated pyramidal roof and finial on top; dormer window.

Marchmont House. ● Probably built in 1750. Single chambered; grey slate cupola; no stringcourse; had a potence.

Mertoun House.* ☉ Oldest dated in Scotland 1576. Designed by Sir William Bruce. Four buttresses; domed roof of smooth stone or cement; wooden louvre. In fine condition, with many doves. (Fig. 1 Frontispiece)

Ninewells House. ● 16th century. Stone slab roof; round hole in roof guarded by rim of iron spikes.

Nisbet House.* ▲ Only pentagonal one in Scotland; wedge-shaped overlapping stone roof with battlemented parapet; pointed arched window over entrance.

Old Mill House, Foulden. ■■ Gables with three tall steps and cote resembles a tower; slated roof. (May have been destroyed.)

Press Castle. ■■ On south wall metal tablet with three mullets and crescents, 1607 T A. Two-storeyed; battlemented walls; merlons and crenelles on south side and gables with sham cannon.

Preston Farm. F. With slated ridge roof on farm buildings; at each angle of roof moulded convex skewput with spiral ends.

Spottiswoode House. ● Ruinous; Two windows with four small rectangular loopholes; porch built on south side; five doors to basement; ogee roof.

Swinton House. ● Tablet dated 1746; wrecked potence; has been repaired.

Upsettlington. F. large tower over arch; two windows with entrance holes; marks of nest boxes.

Whitehall House, Chirnside. ⊞ Large two-chambered; slated lean-to roof with double dormer windows; human face carved on each skewput.

Niven Robertson gives a list of eighteen vanished cotes in Berwickshire.

Aberlady Church. T. Entrance holes now blocked.

Amisfield.* ▲ Like a Greek temple, at S.E. corner of walled garden. (Fig 23).

Athelstaneford.* ▬ dated 1583; in poor condition.

Balgone Barns. T. Old windmill; still frequented by pigeons.

Bankton House. ■ Ground floor was once a cellar.

Belton. ⊟ Corrugated iron roof. In fair repair.

Bielside. T. Old windmill.

Bolton. ● Conical slate roof with louvre.

Bourhouse. ⊟ Arched doorways made in lower storey, for a stable.

Castle Mains. ■ Deteriorating; roofless.

Colstoun House.* ● Excellent example. Well preserved.

Congalton Gardens. ⊙ Recently demolished; probably ancient.

Dirleton Castle.* ⊙ Large and in good condition. (D. of E.)

Dolphingstone. ⊙ Stone slab roof; reasonable repair.

Drylawhill.* ⊙ In fine condition. Tall with slated roof and wooden dormer window. (Fig. 11).

Dunbar, Friarscroft.* ▲ Unusual. In remains of a monastery; in good repair.

East Fortune. ▬ Slated roof; plain gables; stone ball ornaments and weathervane on rear wall.

Elvingston.* ◕ In perfect repair. Battlemented top; potence and sanded floor.

Fountainhall. ◪ Ruinous. Imitation dovecot on other side of cartshed.

Haddington, Crocegate. ■ Fair repair. Remains of ball ornaments and weathervane.

Haddington, Lady Kitty's Garden.* ● In good condition, supposed to be resurrectionist tower. (Fig. 13).

Hailes Castle.* T. Unusual, as in castle and over a dungeon. (D. of E.) (Fig. 7).

Harelaw. F. Well preserved and complete; in farm steading.

Herdmanston. ⊟ Ruinous; in quiet lovely situation.

Heugh, North Berwick. ● Now flat concrete roof; sixteen entrance holes in grid on south side; pigeons.

Humbie ⊟ was converted into cottage in 1971.

Huntington. ▲ Like part of a chapel; sometimes used as a stable.

Johnstounburn.* ⊡ Magnificent cote dated 1730. Only one door to chambers separated by central cylinder; pigeons.

Keith Marischal.* ▲ Upper part of octagonal building; potence; pigeons. In good repair.

Lawhead F dated 1858. Entrance holes over arch.

Letham. ⊡ Disintegrating.

Luffness House. ☉ Old beehive with domed roof and stone louvre.

Luffness House.* T. Water tower, like a campanile.

Meikle Pinkerton.* ☉ Large beehive with conical slated roof; potence; pigeons.

Muirfield Gate. F. Modern one at back of house; pigeons.

New Byth. ⊡ Pleasant Georgian one.

Newtonhall. ■ Ridge roofed; probably ancient. Roof once stone slabs, now corrugated iron. Used as shed.

North Berwick, Abbey. ⊡ Large; stone slab roof. Showing signs of decay.

North Berwick, The Lodge. ■ Slated roof. In relatively good repair.

Nunraw.* ☉ Impressive. Upper part with louvre probably built on old beehive one. (Fig. 12).

Ormiston. ● Tower with parapet; no roof, otherwise in good repair.

Papple F corbelled doocot over arch.

Pencaitland.* ▬ Iron hoops over entrance holes; roof collapsing.

Pencaitland Church. T. Entrance holes in south wall.

Phantassie.* ☉ Once a windmill; has curious horseshoe roof facing south. (N.T.S.) (Fig. 25).

Pilmuir House. ■ Charming cote in good order; pigeons.

Prestonpans, Northfield.* ☉ In excellent state, thanks to County Planning.

Preston Tower. ■ 17th century. Stone ball finials. (Fig. 18) (D. of E.)

Redhouse. ⊡ Lower part a storehouse; vaulted ceiling.

Rockville. F. Circular tower with weathercock on slated roof; potence. Reasonable repair.

Ruchlaw. ⊡ Eighteen entrance holes halfway up slated roof;

33

poor condition.

St Clement's Wells. ■ Dilapidated; nearby site of old gin distillery.

St Germain's. ● Circular parapet; has a potence.

Saltcoats Castle. ■ Roofless; north wall gone.

Saltoun Hall. ▲ Battlemented octagon on square base; used as a store.

Saltoun Home Farm.* F. Octagon with cupola on square base; in farm courtyard. (Fig. 22)

Spott. ☐ 1422 nests; potence.

Stenton Church. T. Arched door in gable; good repair; pigeons. (Fig. 8).

Tantallon Castle.* ☐ Well preserved; Stone slab roof. (D. of E.)

Thurston. ■ Pointed slated roof; pigeons. In good state.

Trabroun. F. At entrance to farm offices; in good order.

Tranent.* near church. ■ Belonged to the Setons dated 1587. Panels on south wall; used to have 2,000 nests; under repair.

Tranent. T. Small one in turret. Now under repair.

Tyninghame House. F. Ridge roof; pigeons.

Waughton. ☉ Old beehive in bad repair; pigeons. (Fig. 4).

Whitburgh House. ● Whitewashed, with conical slated roof and louvre. Good repair.

Whitekirk Church. T. Still has pigeons.

Whittingehame. T. On outbuildings.

MIDLOTHIAN

Addiston House. ☐ In good repair.

Alderstone House. ■■ Roofless and deteriorating; three of five stone ball finials remain.

Bonnington House. ☉ Domed roof. Used as a storehouse.

Bowland House. ■ Used as a coal-store.

Brickswold House, Bonnyrigg. F. Octagonal. In disrepair, entrance holes blocked. Brick.

Burnhouse. ● Ruinous.

Carrington Church. T. In church tower.

Castlesteads. ■■ Ruinous.

Cliftonhall. F. On arch; unfloored circular, with large stone nests.

Costerton House. ■ Ruinous, but still attractive.

Edmonstone House.* ▲ Like a chapel, with small steeple. (Fig. 24).

Eskgrove House. ■ Dilapidated; may be removed for road widening.

Eskhill House. ■ Slated ridge roof; some crowsteps missing; no nest or entrance holes. Made into studio.

Fordel Park. F. On north side of farm court, all that is left are marks of stone steps.

Harburn House. T. Gothic battlemented. In good repair, but some holes in corrugated iron roof.

Hawthornden Castle. ▲ Nest holes in cave.

Inveresk Manor House. ■ pyramidal roof, now a garden house.

Inveresk Gate. ■ Dilapidated.

Linnhouse. ⊓ In good state except for roof, which may soon be reslated.

Locheriot Farm. ■ Becoming derelict.

Loretto School. T. In School buildings.

Malleny House.* ■ Excellent condition; ridge roof. (N.T.S. garden)

Masterton House T. Tower with doocot, demolished about 1960.

Mavisbank. ● Ruinous; no roof.

Newhailes House. ■ Fanlight above entrance; roof and dormer window falling in.

Newton House. ● Original 16th century defence tower. In good condition.

Penicuik House, Arthur's O'on. F. Magnificent with potence; many pigeons. Splendid condition.

Penicuik House, Knight's Law. T. No doves; well preserved, but part of parapet gone.

Pinkie House. ⊓ Well preserved. Large; panels of the Seton family over doors.

Pittendreich House. ■ Ridge-roofed; four large concave skewputs. In good repair, but harling falling off.

Preston Hall. F. Rectangular building over an archway in stable court. No entrance holes.

Ratho Park Golf Course. ⊓ Roofless; once had 1,641 nests.

Over the entrance is 17 AF 13, Alexander Foulis of Ratho.

Ratho Hall. ● Small and quaint.

Ravelrig House. ▬ Relatively good repair.

Rosebery House. F. Basement in clock tower in farmyard.

Sherriffhall. T. Square tower with circular interior; round shot holes in walls.

Thornton Farm, Whitehills.* ■ Large two-storey; built of fine red sandstone.

Vogrie Grange. F. Lectern type, older than surrounding farm buildings: pantile roof.

EDINBURGH

Comiston House. T. Old defence tower with corbelled parapet.

Corstorphine.* ☉ 16th century. Tun-bellied with six openings in flat roof; Socket of potence. Well kept. (D. of E.)

Craighouse. ▬ Ruinous, destroyed by ivy.

Craigmillar Castle. T. 15th century. In round defence tower. (D. of E.)

Drum House. F. Square tower on farm buildings. With lectern roof.

Drumbank House. T. Triangular with base to south; upper part contains doocot built of bricks.

Drylaw. ▬ Large and ruined. Vertical sundial on east coign stone. 'Dovecot Inn' nearby.

East Morningside House. ■ Unusual with roof to north; doveholes in wooden frame in angle of walls.

Granton Castle. ☐☐ Small; once had two chambers; used as Air Raid Shelter in 1939–45 War. Well preserved, no nest holes.

Hermitage of Braid.* ☐☐ Ornate late 17th or early 18th century. Once had five renaissance urns at corners. Repaired; walls pointed; new gutter below roof; windows green-shuttered; entrance holes repaired; finials gone.

Liberton House. ■ 17th century. Almost square.

Liberton Tower. T. Once used as a doocot, with two doveholes in south wall.

Lochend.* ☉ Old beehive in excellent condition.

Merchiston Castle School. ▬ Ruined, with at one time stone slab ridge roof; nest holes well made.

Morton House. ■ Northern of two pavilion houses is a doocot with ogee cupola roof.

Mortonhall House. ■■ Transverse rectangular window; roof slated, as half-cone ending in a ridge.

Nether Liberton.* ⊓⊔ Superb large crowstepped, with pantiled roof; double entrance doors; forty-six entrance holes and 2072 nest holes. (Fig. 2. Frontispiece).

Niddrie Marischal. F. Battlemented back wall. (Not discovered on visit).

Prestonfield House. F. In stable offices. May have gone.

Ravelston House. ⊓⊔ Large; used to have stone baths for birds. Now converted into a house. (Figs. 27 and 28).

Redhall.* ▲ 1756. Fine and unusual. Otterburn coat-of-arms; potence shaped like lyre; pyramidal roof with 9-pointed star.

St Katherine's House. F. Part of old stables; now a storehouse. Particularly large nestholes. Well kept.

Niven Robertson lists fifty-five Edinburgh cotes as having vanished. Since his survey, several others have gone.

WEST LOTHIAN

Auchenard. ■■ Small, ruinous.

Binny House. ■ 18th century. Rubble built with ashlar blocks at corners; pyramidal slated roof with dormer window; twelve wooden entrance holes; many fantail doves.

Blackburn Hall. ■ Roof collapsing; large square nest holes; row of entrance holes cut in stone.

Blackness Castle. ⊓⊔ Demolished except for rear wall. (D. of E.)

Boghead House. ■ Slated roof.

Carmelite Church, South Queensferry. T. Possibly 15th century. Spiral staircase.

Carriden Grange. ■ lectern over arcaded base.

Carriden House. F. Square tower in stables, dated 1818.

Craigiehall House. ■ Roofless; evidence of repairs to walls.

Dechmont House. F. In roof of farm buildings.

Dundas Castle.* ● Excellent condition; double doors; potence.

Foxhall. ■■ Stone ball finial on north east corner and conical stone on rear wall.

Houston House. ⊞ Roofless; east chamber smaller than west.

Humbie. ⊞ Disintegrating; nest partitions 2ft 4ins in width.

Kilpunt House. ● 18th century. Slated conical roof.

Kirkliston Church. T. A few entrance holes in tower.

Linlithgow. ⊙ Large beehive; louvre with ogee dome.

Loch Cote. ■ Base almost square with rounded corners; rubble built; inside lower chamber vaulted roof; upper part mid. 19th century; ashlar blocks. To south horizontal row of stone entrance holes, some now on ground. On upper west wall sculptured cross; no nest holes seen.

Loganlea. ■ Ruins.

Midhope Castle.* ⊞ Fine large cote with 2,003 nest holes; slated roof. (Fig. 6).

Newliston House.* ⊞ Had 2,603 nests; beautiful cote, converted into a house.

Ochiltree Castle. T. Small one in turret; entrance holes now blocked.

Philipstoun House. ⊞ dated 1725. Holes in long dormer window to serve both cotes. In poor condition.

Torbane Hill. ● Removed about 1977.

Wallhouse. ▲ Round arched windows and cruciform recesses; no roof.

Niven Robertson mentions eighteen doocots which have vanished in West Lothian.

LANARKSHIRE

Ampherlaw House. ■ Small, attractive; no crowsteps but has scroll pediments; entrance holes blocked; no access to loft possible.

Auchtifardle. dovecot has gone.

Blackwood House. ⊞ 17th century. Converted into pleasant house. Only 23 nestholes used to hold ornaments. Stone balls on rear wall.

Braidwood (Hallbar Tower.) T. In North wall, doveholes also used as nests; kept warm by chimney flue.

Cadder. ● Dated 1753. Slated conical roof; on golf course.

Cairnhill Hotel. F. Dated 1762. Large cylinder in offices, which are being destroyed by builders. Entrance walls wrecked.

Cambusnethan Priory. ⊏⊐ Blown up by farmer in 1966. No trace remains.

Carmichael House. ● 18th century. Stone slab roof with stone pineapple finial. Flagstone floor. Nestboxes perfect. In good order.

Carnwath, Eastshield. T. 17th century. In tower of old castle; some nestholes remain.

Cleuch House, Wilsontown. ■ Roofless and disintegrating; once had stone ball ornaments on rear wall.

Coltness House. ■ Early 19th century. Ridge roof of scalloped shaped slates.

Corehouse. ■ 17th century. No roof. Ruinous; wide stringcourse.

Covington Castle. ⊙ Probably 16th century. Deteriorating; outer walls falling; tree growing on east side and grass on roof which has no louvre now.

Daldowie House. ● Large well built; ogee roof.

Douglas Support. ■ Ruinous, but charming; red sandstone with large square nestholes.

Drumpellier Old Stables. F. Early 19th century.

Hardington House. F. In stable block.

Lanark. ■ Removed years ago, in Dovecote Lane.

Lee House. ■ Pyramidal roof; projections at each corner.

Libberton. ■ Small slated ridge-roof; may not have been a doocot; three entrance holes with landing ledges blocked; no nest holes.

Muirhousedykes Mains. ■ Near farmhouse.

Murdostoun Castle. ▲ Octagonal; over an icehouse; slated roof with ball ornament. Excellent condition except for ivy.

Orbiston, Bothwell. ■

Rochsoles House. F. 1839. Slated pyramidal roof; horizontal row of entrance holes blocked by wooden beam, but in good order.

Shieldhill House. T. Lancet windows; battlemented top; covered with ivy; no roof.

Torrance Castle. ■ Roofless; badly damaged.

Waygateshaw House. ■ roofless; side walls collapsing. Only 15 nest boxes remain.

Westburn House, Cambuslang. ▲ Octagonal with slated ogee roof; restored; on Westburn Golf Course.

Wishaw House. F. Small square with slated roof.
Niven Robertson lists ten cotes which have gone in
Lanarkshire.

AYRSHIRE

Adrossan Castle. ■■ Roofless; crowstepped. Ladies' lavatory
built on north wall.
Auchinleck House. ■ Red brick.
Crossraguel Abbey.* ⊙ Perhaps once a defence tower. Stone
roof with rectangular opening. (Fig. 5). (D. of E.)
Doonside House. T. Pleasant brick building on arches of pink
sandstone; lean-to roof with battlements. (Fig. 19).
Drumfad. ● 1762. Roofless and decaying.
Dumfries House. ■■ Dated 1671. Slated ridge-roof; two
skewputs with carved human faces. In good order.
Dunure Castle.* ⊙ 16th century. Flat roof; no louvre now. In
good repair. (D. of E.)
Eglinton Castle. early 19th century.
Finnart's Holm. ● Conical slated roof. In good order.
Fullarton House. ■■ 18th century, Ruinous.
Kerelaw House. ■■ 1775. Crowstepped with stone ball fini-
als; slated roof.
Kilmaurs, Tour. early 19th century.
Kilmaurs, south of Parish Church. 1636.
Lanfine House.
Monkton.* T. Old windmill in good order. Conical slated roof;
brick pigeon holes.
Sundrum House. Only ruins remain.

Kilkerran House. The late Sir James Fergusson informed
me that there used to be a cote in a field near the house called
Ducat Field. He had a painting by John Wilson of the 1820's
showing a pagoda-like doocot with the house in the distance.

Culzean Castle. Local employees say that the small building
at the side of the stables looking over the sea was once a
doocot, and one of them said that carrier pigeons brought
messages here. Now there is no evidence of it having been
one.

RENFREWSHIRE

Capelrig,* Deaconsbank Golf Course. ● Possibly 17th century. Stone roof; well maintained by Golf Club.

Craigends Castle, Houston. T. Once used for fancy pigeons, and as a water tower.

Erskine. F. Loft in stable buildings; a few nest holes. May possibly be restored.

Newark Castle.* ⊙ Conical stone roof; old latrine in basement. Good repair. (D. of E.)

Pollok Castle. ■ ■ 17th century. Twin Cotes at corner of garden; slated roofs with louvre.

'Wallace House', Elderslie. ■ West room of upper storey.

White House of Milliken, Kilbarchan.* T. Was whitewashed; no roof; pleasant cornice.

A. Niven Robertson has notes of six cotes now gone.

GLASGOW

Pollockshaws. T. Red brick with conical slated roof; no nests; 'Dovecote Cottage' nearby.

DUNBARTONSHIRE

Camus Eskan. ▲ late 17th or early 18th century. Octagonal; no roof; disintegrating.

Cumbernauld. ● Basement used as henhouse; potence imperfect.

Darleith, Cardross. T. About 1790. Conical slated roof. In good repair.

Douglaston House, Milngavie. ▲ Hexagonal; roofless; no potence now.

Dunglass Castle. ⊙ Concrete roof.

Gartshore House. 18th century.

Geilston House. ■ 18th century. In good repair.

Mains Farm, Bearsden. F. On top of farm building.

Strathleven House. ■■ 18th century. Pedimented.

A. Niven Robertson records two cotes which have vanished in Dunbartonshire.

STIRLINGSHIRE

Arnprior. ■ Red brick; roofless.

Arnotdale House. ▲ dated 1834. Vertical sundial. Fantail pigeons.

Avondale House. F. Battlemented tower over stone archway.

Bannockburn House.* ■ Dated 1708. Tall, ruined but still elegant; vertical sundial; 1,169 nests.

Balquatston House. F. Over pend. In good repair.

Boquhan House. Early 19th century.

Callander House. F. Square battlemented tower in stables; seven entrance holes.

Cambuskenneth Abbey. ⊡ Ruinous; only parts of two walls remain; still some nest holes.

Carron House. ▲ Big brick cote; sandstone course; entrance and doveholes; ruinous.

Craigmaddie House. ● Ruinous.

Drumquhossle. ▰

Drymen. ▰ 1711.

Dunipace House. ▲ Tiled nest holes.

Dunmore House. F. Square; over pend; wooden nests.

Easter Livilands. F. Octagonal over archway; no nests or doveholes; fox as finial. Has vanished. Location now a housing estate.

Gargunnock House. ▲ Covered with ivy; domed roof.

Herbertshire House. F. At farm court.

Muiravonside House. ▰ 17th century. Two unusual dormer windows with landing ledges; one dormer window facing east. Poor condition.

Neuk House. F. Octagonal tower in offices; modern tiled roof with arrow weathervane.

Old Polmaise. ● Early 18th century. Slated cupola roof; possessed a potence ? demolished, not found in November 1979.

Park Hall, Killearn. ▲ 18th century.

Park Hill, Grangemouth. ▰ 18th century.

Powis House. F. Octagonal tower in farm court; cupola roof.

Powfoulis House. T. Tiny.

Sauchie House. ⊡ Dilapidated; vertical window in west gable.

South Bantaskine. ▲ Used to be beautiful, but demolished years ago.

Stenhouse. F. 19th century. Octagonal; over entrance to stables.

Touch House. ■ Rectangular window over entrance; corrugated iron roof.

Westquarter.* ■ Shield with date 1647. Back wall has triple curve with stone balls. Perfectly restored. (D. of E.)

A. Niven Robertson mentions twenty-one which have vanished in Stirlingshire.

CLACKMANNAN

Alva House. F. Ruinous square tower in stable court.

Brucefield. F. 18th century. Square tower with pantiled roof on stables, with louvre.

Kennet House. F. Octagonal on former stable: may have vanished.

Kilbagie. ● Dated 1859. Roofless; survivor of a pair of circular towers. A few brick nests remain.

Newmills Crossing. ■ 17th century. Unusual crowsteps; roof falling in.

Sauchie. T. Converted windmill with battlemented walls and peculiar red brick recesses.

KINROSS

Dowhill Castle. T. Roofless round barmekin tower of old castle.

Kinross House. F. In centre of farm court; cupola roof with louvre and weathervane; ? potence.

Lethangie House. ■ Attractive dormer windows; pyramidal slated roof.

Tullibole Castle. Dated 1751. Roofless and no remaining nestholes.

A Niven Robertson records two vanished cotes in Kinross.

Aberdour Castle.* ⊙ 16th century. Well kept. (D. of E.)

Aberdour, Hillside. ⊙ 16th century. Probably vanished.

Aberdour, Main Road.* ● Still there; wrecked by children, doorway now repaired.

Anstruther Manse. ■ 17th century. Roof slated.

Ardross Castle. ■■

Auchtermuchty, McDuff. ■■ Reroofed with corrugated asbestos; now only three entrance holes; many doves.

Balcarres House. ■ Tile nests; pyramidal roof.

Balcaskie House.* ● ● Twin cotes with potences; designed by Sir Robert Lorimer.

Ballingall. ■■ Door in east wall.

Balmerino, Birkhill Home Farm. F. In central pediment.

Balmule. ■■ Ruinous.

Balram. ■■ Dated 1688. Ruinous.

Blackhall, Tulliallan. ■■ On estate buildings.

Bogward.* ⊙ 16th century, Repaired.

Bordie ☐☐ Only one entrance door; roofless; west chamber collapsed

Brunton Barns, Markinch. ■ Roofless.[1]

Burntisland, Grange. ■■ Once a dwelling house with windows, now used as store.

Caiplie. ■■ Dated 1735. Roofless, once thatched.

Cambo House. ▲ Late 17th century. Octagonal, with battlemented top.

Cambo Farm. F. Battlemented tower on farm buildings.

Cambo Stables. F. Conical roof.

Carberry, N. of Kirkcaldy.[1]

Carnbee. ■■ Roofless.

Carphin House. ■ Restored, with potence.

Carriston. ☐☐ Only one entrance door; slated roof.

Carslogie Castle. ■■ Corrugated iron roof.

Cartmore. ● N. of Lochgelly.[1] Pigeons.

Charleton House. ■■ Becoming derelict; rare entrance holes cut in stone; partly in dormer, partly in front wall.

Colinswell. ■■ Decaying; coloured red from aluminium works.

Corston Tower. T. Now a fragment, only part of one wall.

Craigfoodie House. F. Much altered, on garden wall.

Crail, Barns. ■ Reroofed with pantiles; buttresses. Still used.

Crail, Hollowflat. ⊙ Probably 16th century.

Creich Castle. ■ Dated 1723. In farm steading.

Cupar, garden in Ashlar. ■ Roofless; altered; used as shed.

Dairsie Castle. T. At south west angle of castle; six oval gun loops.

Denbrae House. ☐☐ Dated 1706. Ruined.

Denmuir Farm. ☐☐ Dated 1724. Slated roof.

Dewar's Mill, St Andrews ☐☐ Dated 1754. Slated roof.

Doo Cave, Wemyss.* ▲ A series of entrance holes above a blocked-up entrance.

Dron House. ■ Roofless.

Drumfin Farm. ● Reslated; potence.

Drums Farm. ■ Below a Maltese Cross the date 1738.

Dunino House

Dura House. ■ Dated 1728. Small; covered with ivy.

Durie House.* T. Octagonal, with concave curve, resting on plinth; potence; recently repaired.

Dysart House. ⊙ Exterior sound; interior ruinous.

Dysart, St Serf's Church. ■ Ruinous; view of it obscured by public lavatory.

Earlshall House.* ■ Dated 1599. Ornate and fine; angled openings in sides. Repaired.

East Forthar. ■ Ruined.

East Grange, Culross. ■ Back wall has two stone ball ornaments.

East Kincaple. ■

East Luscar House.* ■ Dated 1678. Ridge roof with red pantiles, Dilapidated.

East Newbeith Farm, Kingsbarns. F. Part of farm steading as attractive tower.

Edenshead.* ■ Beautiful. Repaired by owner with help from Anc. Mon. Comm.

Elie House. ● Ball finial on false louvre.

Falkland Palace. T. Near old Pell-Mell court; stone slab roof. (N.T.S.)

Fernie Castle. ■ Dated 1661. Roofless.

Fernwoodlee. ● Roofless; crenellated top. No nest boxes. Harled inside.

Fingask Farm. ■■ Slate and stone roof.

Foodie Farm. ■ Small.

Glen Duckie. ■■ Slated roof.

Grange of Balmerino. ■ Ruinous.

Grange of Kirkcaldy. ■■ Dilapidated.

Gregston, Cameron. ☐☐ Ruinous.

Hill House, Dunfermline. ● once a windmill, never a doocot despite marked as such on old O.S. Map.

Inchcolm Abbey. T. Crude nestholes in central tower; probably ancient.

Inchrye. F. Derelict square tower at stables.

Innergellie.* ☐☐ 17th century. Harled rubble with remains of pantile roof.

Inverkeithing, 50 High Street. ■■ Removed about 1970.

Inverkeithing, Bank House. ■ Ruinous, covered with ivy. Remains of stringcourse. No nestboxes.

Inverkeithing, Rosebery House. ■■ Some of upper part removed. Corrugated iron roof sloping from front to back. Otherwise in good order with nestboxes, some used for holding tools. Now an oil store.

Keavil, Dunfermline (Martha Frew Home). ■■ Destroyed by Council some years ago.

Kellie Castle. F. No true doocot, but pigeon holes set above shed. (N.T.S.)

Kemback House. ☐☐ Dated 1710. Ruinous.

Kenley Green, Boarhills. ■■ Ridge roof with louvre.

Kilconquhar House. ☐☐ Walls of harled rubble; three entrance holes below stringcourse.

Kilmaron House. F. Over stable pend.

Kilry. ■■ Dated 1684. Handsome.

Kinaldy House. ■■ Corrugated asbestos roof.

Kincardine House. F. Attached to sheds; corrugated iron roof, with some pantiles.

Kincraig, Elie ■■ Crowstepped with dormer.[1]

Kinghorn, Bow Butts.* ■ Square base, with octagonal upper part; most attractive with slated octagonal roof and finial.

Kinloch, Collessie. ● Conical slate roof.

Kinnaird. ■■ 1705. Ruinous.

Kippo. ■■ Dated 1706. Pantiled roof. Needs some repair.

Kirkforthar Farm. ⊙ Ruinous; unusual sloping roof.

Kirkton House, Forgan. ■ Ruinous.

Lahill House. ■ Ruinous.

Langside. N. of Kennoway ■ – ruined.[1]

Largo House. ■ Roofless.

Largo Tower. T. Doocot in top storey of defence tower; conical slated roof deteriorating.

Lathrisk House. ■

Letham Village (1) ■ Ruinous, but still has doves.

Letham Village (2) ■ Small; restored; doves.

Leuchars Castle.* ● 1661. Fine and ornate. Deteriorating.

Logie House. ■ 18th century. Pyramidal roof; renovated.

Lochmalony House. ■ 17th century. Roof gone.

Lundin Tower. ▲ Like a chapel with gothic windows.

Macduff's Castle. ⊙ 16th century. Stone roof.

Melville House. ● Unusual; once a windmill; in good condition with potence.

Montrave House. ⊡ Pleasant with pantiled roof.

Mountquhanie Castle. (1) F. Joined to farm buildings; (2) F. Over court of offices; (3) T. Lower Part of small round tower.

Mount Melville House. ⊡ Red tiled roof. Now a byre.

Naughton House. ⊡ dated 1750.

Nether Rankeillour. ⊡ Slated roof.

Newark Castle. ⊙ 16th century. Stone roof.

Newton of Kingsdale, Kennoway. ■ Ruinous.

North Glassmount. ■

Nydie Farm. ⊡ Late 17th century; rebuilt about 1800. Entrances in sides. Now ruinous.

Old Whitehills. ■ Derelict.

Parbroath. ■ Ruinous.

Pitcormie House. F. In farm court.

Pitcullo Castle. ■ Ruinous.

Pitcorthy House. F. Octagonal tower in court. Not found in 1977.

South Pitdinny. ■ With potence.

Pitlour. F. Rectangular over pend in stable offices.

Pitreavie House. ■ Roofed. (D. of E.)

Pittencrieff Park. ● Deteriorating, with masonry crumbling and some battlements missing. No nestboxes, but some iron

47

spikes no doubt used as supports for wooden nests.

Prestonhall House. ■ Roofless; no stringcourse on back; on east and west sides two entrance holes with landing ledges.

Pyeston Farm. ▭ Roofless but still used by pigeons.

Raith House. ■

Rathillet House. ■ Stone ornaments; potence; cubical sundial.

Renniehill House.* ■ Dated 1625. Round gunloop in rear wall.

Rosyth Castle.* ■ Old ridge roof; faces carved on skewputs of gables. (D. of E.)

Rumgally. ■ 1,021 sandstone nests, pantiled roof.

St Andrews, St Mary's. T. Slated roof.

St Andrews, 46 South Street. ■ Square turret with two stone ball ornaments; entered by a ladder.

St Andrews, Bute Memorial Hall. ▭ – double slated roof with horizontal row of entrance holes. In good order.

St Fort House. ▭ 1735. Has been restored.

Sands House. ■ Ruinous.

Scotscraig. ■ Somewhat dilapidated.

Scotstarvit.* T. Built as one in top chamber of tower. (D. of E.)

South Dron, Leuchars.

Stoneywind, Boarhills. ■ No roof; ruinous.

Strathairly House. ■ Good condition. Steep crowsteps and Z-shaped stringcourse; slated roof.

Strathendry Castle. ■ At farm offices.

Strathtyrum. ■ Slated roof; broken potence. Needs some repair, on pediment initials and "repaired 1812".

Struthers Castle. ■ Ruinous.

Tarvit Mill. ■ Roofless; decaying; vertical split in rear wall; stone entrance holes.

Thirdpart Farm. ■ Now used as a cart shed.

Todhall Farm. T. Battlemented.

Transy House. ■ Now a "rickle of stones".

Walton. ■ Slated roof.

Wemyss Castle. ● Battlemented top with merlons; ? potence.

Wemyss Hall (Hill of Tarvit).* ● Battlemented top with inclined roof; potence. (N.T.S.)

West Grange House, Culross. ■ Roofless. Nest boxes complete. Lintel dated 1761.

West Pitkierie Farm.* T. 1782. Charming and ornate with concave outer faces; battlemented parapet with stone vases.

Wormiston. ■ 2-storeyed, with slated roof.

A. Niven Robertson listed the names of sixty-seven cotes which have vanished; since then the Ancient Monuments Commission (Department of the Environment) refers to twenty-three in addition.

[1] mentioned by Mr Smail.

PERTHSHIRE

Abercairney House. ■ Probably 17th century. Ruinous.

Arthurstone House. ■ 1883. Ruinous.

Auchleeks House. F. About 1820. In stable block; pyramidal roof.

Auchterarder House. F. 1833. Over pend in stables.

Ayton House nr. Abernethy F. In steading.

Balendoch House. ■ Early 19th century. Pyramidal roof. Recently whitewashed. Some pigeons.

Balhary. F. Doocot in west gable of stables; red sandstone; stone floor with stone trap door for dung; about 260 wooden nests.

Ballathie House. ■ Small.

Ballindean House. F. Square; slated ogee roof. No entrance holes.

Bandirran House. ■ Roof partly slated; partly tiled.

Barnhill. F. Small square one in steading with brick or wood nests.

Bonhard House. ☐☐ 1709. Slated roof and fourteen arched openings.

Cardross. T. Like a pagoda.

Carey. F. In steading.

Castle Huntly.* ■ Quaint; only West turret at corner remains. Falling into disrepair.

Castle Menzies. T. Possible doocot in tower.

Dunbarny House. ■ Lintel dated 1697. Three round windows; red tiled roof; no doveholes.

49

Dunbarrow. F. 18th century. Loft.

Duncrievie. F. Loft in farm steading with pantiled roof.

Duncrub House. ■■ Marriage lintel dated 1725. Slated ogee roof with weathercock. Excellent order in garden of St Andrews' Cottage.

Ecclesmagirdle (Glenearn House). ● Harled with unusual doveholes. Roof needs some repair. Ancient.

Elcho Castle. ☉ 16th century. No louvre or doveholes. (D. of E.)

Fingask Castle. ■ About 1770. – not found on visit.

Findgask, Chapel Bank. F. Disappeared when new farm buildings erected.

Gask House. T. Part of the old house; thatched roof with weathercock. Thatch needs some repair.

Glencarse. F. Square one at steading.

Glendoick House. ■ 18th century. Whitewashed; dormer window; entrance holes in south and west walls; conical slated roof, with weathervane falling.

Glentarkie. ■■ Ruinous.

Huntingtower Hotel. F. In outbuildings; eighteen entrance holes; two rectangular windows on either side; red tiled roof.

Inchmartine House. F. Domed cote over arch of farm offices.

Inverardoch Mains. ● With battlements.

Invererne House. F. At farm steading.

Invermay House. ▲ 18th century. Roofless; octagonal; red sandstone with stone corbels.

Jordanstone. F. Pleasant one above garage

Keithick House. F. At stables over elliptical arch.

Kilgraston School. ■■ Pulled down by farmer about 1963.

Killiechassie. T. Gothic 1850. In good order.

Kilspindie.* ■■ 3 Unusual dormers; slated roof; 1,544 nests. In poor repair

Kincarrochy House.* ■■ Dated 1694. Stone slab roof; arched stone entrances.

Kinloch (on Bankhead of Kinloch). F. Red sandstone ashlar over archway, with peeling whitewash; slated roof; stringcourse; rectangular window, with no small entrance holes; doves use it; high door to north but entrance not feasible.

Kinmonth House.* ☐☐ 2,364 nests; twenty-five arched openings in dormer window in slated roof; three crowstepped hoods with finials on back wall. In good order.

Kinnaird Castle. ■■ Oblong stone on back wall. Pigeons. Well cared for.

Kippenross. ● 18th century. Corbelled parapet and small open cupola; ball finial and weathervane. Has been repaired.

Knapp, Hilltown of –* ☐☐ Three finials; triangular crowstepped back walls. Converted into a cottage. Charming.

Megginch Castle.* ▲ Hexagonal on six pointed arches over a well; potence; hexagonal roof bearing three-masted ship finial. (Fig. 16).

Moncrieffe House. ■■ 1729. Roofless.

Mylnefield. F. Small one in offices.

Newbigging. ■■ circ. 1730.

Newhouse. F. Early 19th century. In attic of steading.

Newton of Condie. ■■ 17th century. Roofless ruin.

Old Potento Mill. F. Former mealmill with pend, became doocot in circ. 1878, repaired in 1963. Now disintegrating, and no sign of entrance or nest holes.

Pitfour Castle. ☐☐ 2,087 nests; three pedestals for stone balls; double entrance doors; slated roof falling in.

Piturcarty. F. In steading.

Polcalk.* ☐☐ Probably 17th century. Crenellated back wall; stone slab roof with two small windows; rubble built and white-washed; two doors, one on the left facing west, and the right one facing south; nest holes unusual, horizontal stone slabs with boulders vertically. Good condition except for small holes in roof.

Rednock House. ▲ Octagonal with six arched recesses; cupola roof with weathervane.

Rohallion. Not seen; reference Douglas Sutherland; 'Rohallion'; Heinemann; 1978. p. 48.

Rossie House.* ▲ Handsome hexagonal cote; concave walls; parapet with turrets; quatrefoil window above entrance.

St Martin's. F. Tower on stable roof.

Seggieden. F. Dated 1838. Ornate octagonal building in farm offices. Not found, may have gone.

Tullybelton House. F. Pyramidal roof in centre bay.

Waterybutts. ☐☐ 1733. Back wall had three stone balls on

pedestals; dilapidated slated roof. Outer doors iron, inner ones grilles.

A. Niven Robertson reported nineteen cotes as having vanished in Perthshire.

ANGUS

Abbeythune. F. Early 19th century. Octagonal tower.

Aberlemo. ▲ 18th century. Garden house with privy; doocot in upper storey.

Affleck Castle. F. Square with pyramidal slated roof; nest boxes in good condition.

Anniston (Cotton of Inchock). 17th century. Ruinous.

Ardovie. ■■ Zig-zag stringcourse.

Auchterhouse. ⊓⊓ Front wall has pilaster coigns; two dormer windows; stone slab roof.

Balbinny. ■ Dated 1797. Slated roof repaired.

Baldovie. ■■ Late 18th or early 19th century.

Balgavies. ■■ Whitewashed, no crowsteps; stone slab roof; six peculiar doveholes in roof. Demolished in 1978.

Ballumbie. T. Southernmost corner of tower.

Balmuir. ■■ 18th century. Pantiled roof. In good order.

Balnamoon House.* ⊓⊓ About 1690. Attractive. Stone slab roof at one time now roofless; Stone ball finials; 1,200 nest holes.

Barns of Wedderburn. ● Early 17th century. Roofless.

Boath. ? Probably 17th century. Only vague remains.

Bonnyton. ■■ Once ridge-roofed. Foundations only remain.

Brigton.* ■ 18th century. Two-storey classic with rubble slate pedimented roof and lean-to wings.

Burnside. ■■ Dated 1679 and 1884 on skews. Restored in 1939.

Careston Castle.* ⊓⊓ Surrounded by a moat. Lintel dated 1672. Stone slab roof; 1,390 nest holes, some grey sandstone, some brick.

Claverhouse, Barns of. Two remaining columns.

Cortachy. F. In stable block; some wooden nest boxes remain; wooden floor under stone slabs.

Craigo House. F. Early 19th century. Three-storey on coachhouses.

Denside House. ■■ Neat but with corrugated iron roof.

Downie Mill. ■■ 17th century. Skewputs with carvings of human heads now in miller's garden. Ruinous.

Dumbarrow Mains. T. Old windmill; no nest holes.

Dunninald Castle Mains. F. Square tower with pyramidal roof.

Edzell Castle Mains.* ■■ About 1600, unorthodox. Stone slab ridge-roof; windows with landing ledges; round turret at north-west corner.

Farnell Castle. ■■ Ruinous. (Fig. 20)

Finavon.* ☐☐ Largest in Scotland, 42ft 4 ins by 22ft 4ins; next to Newliston in number of nest holes; stone slab roof, walls cracking but repaired to become Angus Doocot Museum, by Angus Historical Society.

Fornethy. ▲ Hexagonal with slated roof, below which are entrance holes; no nest boxes.

Fothringham House.* ● Unusual, with cattleshed built round it; louvre has gone. Dilapidated.

Gallary House. ☐☐ Green slate roof; 1,236 nest holes; two dormer windows up to eaves.

Gayfield. F. Harled; pyramidal slated roof with weathercock; wooden entrance holes.

Glamis Castle.* ☐☐ Triangular crow-stepped back wall; two dormer windows. Repaired in 1971. (Fig. 17).

Hospitalfield.* ■■ Stone slab roof and flagstone floor; three ball finials.

Keillor House. ■■ 17th century. Hidden in trees.

Kellie Castle.* ■■ 17th century. Stone slab roof; dormer louvre gone on ridge roof. Tree growing above door destroying wall.

Kincaldrum House. ■ Slated ridge-roof; unusual entrance holes.

Kinblethmont House. F. Hexagonal on square tower; entrance holes below slated roof; stone and brick nest holes.

Kingennie, Laws of F. Entrance holes in three parallel vertical rows.

Kinnaber House. ■■ Ridge-roof; nest holes beautifully made. Recently repaired.

Kinnettles House. ■■ Small cote with doveholes in dormer window and in east gable.

Letham Grange. ■ 17th century. Stone roof. In reasonable shape.

Lintrose House. ■ 1797. No roof.

Little Keithock. ■ White-washed with later pyramidal roof; crests on walls.

Lour House. ☐☐ One entrance widened for one chamber to be used as a cart shed; only 100 nest holes left; otherwise in good repair.

Lunan House. ■ Pyramidal slated roof with broken louvre. Also a Doo Cave at Lunan Bay.

Murroes House. ● Early 17th century. Roofless.

Nether Dysart. ■ 17th century. Disintegrating.

Newtonmill.* ■ 18th century. Well kept, Whitewashed; single row of entrance holes.

North Mains of Turin. ■ 17th century. Roofless ruin.

Pearsie House. F. 19th century. On south range of stables. Has gone.

Pitairlie Farm. ■ Probably 17th century. Ruinous.

Pitkerro House. ■ Much damaged by vandals.

Pitmuies House.* ▲ Coat of arms dated 1643. Very fine; two semicircular turrets at corners with cruciform windows; pointed arched entrance.

Pitscandly House. ■ 17th century. Slated roof. In good order, used as garden shed.

Powis Farm House.* ■ Brick on stone plinth; brick nest holes; roof pyramidal, on one side stone slabs, on the others corrugated iron.

Ravensby. ■ Harled with slated roof; carved faces on skewputs, one damaged.

Rochelhill Farm.* ■ Panel dated 1565, with date 1715 on jambs. Slated roof with triangular dormer.

Rosemill Cottage.* ■ Most unusual bow-front; dove holes in triangular dormer. Well cared for.

Rosemount Farm. F. Tower structure in farm buildings.

Stracathro Hospital. F. Octagonal tower in offices; potence; roof has pole finial.

Strathmartine. ■ About 1785. Arched lower storey with doocot above; pyramidal roof.

Strathmartine Glebe. ☐☐

Tealing.* ■ Dated 1595. Stone slab roof and stone floor.

In excellent order. (D. of E.)

Usan House. F. Ogee roof.

Wester Denoon. ■■ Dated 1711.

Westhall. ■■ 17th century. Ruinous.

Woodhill Farm. F. Round tower of farm buildings; used by pigeons.

Woodhill House. ■■ Interesting but roofless. Has been tidied.

Woodrae. ■■ 17th century. Roofless; overgrown.

Within the past twenty years, at least twelve doocots have vanished.

KINCARDINESHIRE

Arbuthnott House. ■ Ruinous.

Arbuthnott Home Farm.* F. Square tower in farm court with no less than seventy-two entrance holes. Still used.

Balbegno Castle.* ■■ Attractive with stone slab roof; no nests.

Balmakewan House. ■ ■ Twin cotes with dormer windows on south-east. In excellent repair and still used.

Banchory Golf Course.* ■ Wooden stave buildings on granite base; ogee pyramidal slated roof. Still used.

Banchory House. ■■

Benholm. ■ Unpretentious with slated pyramidal roof and well made nests.

Blairs College. F. late 18th century.

The Burn. F. On pleasant office court. Fantail pigeons, despite hawks.

Crathes Castle.* ■ Square holes in west wall; conical slated roof with weathervane and metal pigeon. (N.T.S.)

Durris House. F. In stables. Octagonal tower with conical roof carrying weathervane and metal arrow.

Fettercairn House.

Fetteresso Castle.* ☉ 15th century. Large beehive. Still in reasonable repair.

Glenbervie House. 1730.

Hatton Farm. ☐☐ No roof; once had pedestals. Dead pigeons found on floor, perhaps killed by pesticide.

Inglismaldie House. ⊏⊐ Roof falling in, becoming derelict.

Monboddo House. ■ Ruinous red brick on sandstone base.

Muchalls Castle.

Phesdo House.* T. Attractive building; conical slated roof in good repair and with many pigeons.

Pitarrow. ■ Plain with pyramidal slated roof.

A. Niven Robertson mentions four which have gone in Kincardine.

ABERDEENSHIRE

Aberdour House. ■ 1740. Pyramidal roof collapsed.

Aberdour Beach House Hotel. ■ 16th to 17th century. Collapsed.

Aden House. F. In stable yard.

Asloun.* T. Round defence tower with stringcourse, but no roof and no pigeon holes.

Auchaber. ● About 18th century. Conical roof.

Auchenachy Castle. 18th century. With modern slated roof.

Auchenclech. F. In steading; battlemented cote.

Auchencruive. F. Over central arch in steading.

Auchernach.* ● Large cylinder in good repair; conical slated roof.

Auchmacoy.* ⊙ Finest in this county. Barrel-shaped with rectangular top with ridge-roof. In good repair. (Fig. 15).

Auchnacoy, Mill of ▲ About 1800. Octagonal with conical roof.

Auchry House. ● 1767. Circular.

Balmoor. F. 18th century. Large circular building in farm steading. In good condition.

Barra Castle.

Blackford. F. 17th century. Square; conical roof.

Blackhill. F. Ruinous.

Braco Park. F. Late 18th or early 19th century. Slated pyramidal roof.

Byth. ▲ Early 18th century. Octagonal.

Cairngall House. ■ Round arched door with date panel 1811.

Candacraig House. 17th century.

Cluny Home Farm. F. 1860. In Farm buildings. Machicolated tower.

Coburty Mains.

Collieston, Mill of ■ Small pantiled outhouse.

Corsindae. ▬ Late 17th century. Ridge roof of corrugated iron; stone boxes.

Countesswells. ● Tile boxes on brick base; conical roof falling in.

Craig House. ▬ 18th century. Ruinous.

Craigiebuckler.* ▲ Octagonal red brick; brick nests with stone floors; red slated conical roof; potence.

Craigston House. ■ In good state with ridge-roof, dormer and skylight to east.

Crimonmogate.* ▲ 18th century. Octagonal. In good repair. Brick and tile boxes; potence.

Culter House. ■ ■ Circ. 1730. Pyramidal roofs. East one now garden shed.

Davidston, Mains of F. late 18th century. In courtyard.

Delgaty Castle.* ☉ 1570. Triple cylinder; conical stone roof in poor repair.

Disblair House. ▬ Tiny cote with slated ridge-roof; no dormers now.

Drumblade (Newtongarrie). ■ 18th century. Slated pyramidal roof.

Drumblair. ● About 18th century. Conical roof.

Drumrossie. F. 19th century. Square; at farm buildings; corrugated iron roof.

Drums, Foveran. ● Late 18th century. Corrugated iron roof.

Dunecht House. F. At home farm.

Elrick House. ● 16th century. Roofless.

Faichfield. ▬ Late 18th century. Brick lined; roofless.

Fetterletter. ● ● Late 18th century. Twin circular ones.

Fetternear. F. Square tower with pyramidal roof.

Findrach House. ● Conical roof with finial.

Fyvie Castle. F. Early 19th century. Square tower over entrance to farm offices; conical slated roof.

Gartly. ☉ Three stringcourses; crude broken nests.

Gight Castle. ▬ Late 18th or early 19th century.

Glenkindie House.* ▬ 17th century. Slated ridge-roof; crowstepped gables; ball finials; dormer; two slate stringcourses; remains of potence.

Glenmillan House. ● 19th century. Conical roof with dentilled cornice; wooden boxes.

Glentanar House. Not found in June 1978; not known by factor's office.

Grandhome House. ■■ 17th century.

Hatton Castle. F. Early 19th century. Cote in dome of farm offices.

Housedale. F. Mid 18th century. Doocot above dairy. Not found in 1979.

Huntly Castle. F. Cylindrical in centre of farm buildings; had a potence.

Little Idoch. 17th century. Roofless.

Inverwhomery. ● ● ● Early 19th century. Group of three. Conical slated roofs with cupolas and little gothic spires.

Keithfield. ⊙ Only ruins remain.

Kemnay House. ⊙ Ruinous.

Kinaldy House. ■■ Early 18th century with more recent slated roof which is ridge type.

Kininmonth. ■ 18th century. Once had pyramidal roof and wooden boxes.

Kinmundy House. ■ 18th century with pyramidal roof. Has been renovated. Toolshed in lower part.

Kirkton House. ■ Small, in upper storey. Has been restored.

Knockhall Castle. ● Once 16th century bartizan tower. Base only left.

Lessendrum House.* ● Two windows above entrance; slated roof falling in.

Linton, Mains of F. 1835. At outhouses; church-like with pyramidal roof.

Logie Buchan. ● 1838.

Logie Elphinstone House. ■ Square entrance holes in gables with landing ledges; roof deteriorating.

Manar House.* ● In excellent order with louvre; arched window in south wall; situated in lovely garden.

Mansefield, Ellon. Only stump remains.

Meldrum House.* F. Dated 1628. Lovely cote over stable archway with large coat of Royal Scottish Arms; also prayer in Latin.

Memsie.

Midmar, Barns of ■■ 18th century. Remains of rectangular cote.

Mounie Castle. ■ Dated 1694. Restored by Sir Robert Lorimer in 1898 as garden house.

Mounthooly. ▲ 1750. Corbelled, crenellated parapet with twelve ball finials.

Mountpleasant House. ● Early 19th century. Brick gothic with corbelled, crenellated parapet.

Murtle, Mains of ▲ Late 18th century. Pear-shaped.

Orrock Mains. ● circa 1782.

Philorth House. ▲ circa 1800. Brick interior.

Pitcaple Castle. T. In small turret of castle; twenty-four pigeon holes.

Pitlurg Castle. ■ 12ft square; potence pole; conical, slated Victorian roof with ball finial.

Pitsligo.

Pittrichie House. F. Early 19th century. Gothic.

Slains Castle. ■ 1800. Brick, red tile roof; no boxes.

Slains Manse. ● Tiny and roofless.

Smithyhillock. Early 19th century.

Strichen House. ● About 1821. Once had lead dome.

Tillery House. F. At home farm.

Tolquhoun Castle. ▬ A ruin with a few nests remaining. (D. of E.)

Tolquhoun, Newseat of ● ● Small attractive twin cotes; ogee-shaped roofs.

Turnerhall. ■ Dated 1787. Ruinous.

Wardhouse. F. About 1835. Large square tower at home farm.

Whitehill House. Early 19th century. Brick gothic. Ruinous.

Williamston House. F. Early 19th century. In courtyard. Weathervane.

Woodhead. ● Small with no roof.

BANFFSHIRE

Ballindalloch Castle.* ⬚⬚ Tablet over entrance B. 1696. Slated ridge-roof with central louvre; single entrance.

Barnyards of Findlater. Probably 16th century. Rock floor.

Boyne Castle.

Clunie House. Early 19th century. Ruinous.

Durn House.

Edinglassie, Glass. ▢▢ May have been two-chambered. Ruinous.

Forglen House. ■ Brick with conical slated roof and remains of louvre.

Glassaugh House. F. At farm.

Greenbank, Rathven. ● Late 18th century.

Hazelwood. ■ Early 19th century. Harled brick; slated pyramidal roof.

Kininvie House. ● 18th century. Conical roof.

Kinnairdie Castle. Late 18th century.

Leitchiston. ■ Stone roof with four dormer windows and lozenge-shaped holes in gables; divided into four compartments.

Mountblairy House. F. Tower over archway to offices; slated ridge-roof; wooden nests.

Mountbletton Farm. F. Mid 19th century.

Mountcoffer House. ● No roof; on north and south sides cross and circle recesses.

Netherdale House. ● Dated 1774. Circular type in farmyard; potence and gallows; conical slated roof, with dilapidated louvre.

Northfield, Gamrie. Early 19th century.

Recletich, Glenrinnes. ■■ Derelict.

Rothiemay House. ▢▢ Square and two-chambered; tall dormer windows; corrugated iron roof.

Sandyhills, near Banff.* ▲ Hexagonal with battlemented top; nests also in central column.

Seafield, Mains of, Cullen. ■ Ridge roof; garden store on ground floor.

A. Niven Robertson mentions the names of five cotes now vanished in Banffshire.

MORAYSHIRE

Blackhills. ⊙ Ruinous.

Burgie. ■■ Two stringcourses, lower one almost gone; entrance holes in roof.

Burnside. ▲ Octagonal with cupola roof; no nest holes. In good order.

Deanshaugh, Elgin. ■ 18th century.

Findrassie. ■ Dated 1631. In poor shape.

Gordonstoun. T. Converted windmill; entrance through stone vaults; potence with long ladder.

Gordonstoun. ☉ 16th century. Large beehive with three stringcourses.

Grange Hall. ▲ Hexagonal; slated roof and weathervane; four entrance holes in each wall.

Grange Hill. (Dalvey). ■ Ridge-roof; two stringcourses. In poor order.

Invererne. F. Dated 1818. In farm offices; Doric pilasters at corners.

Knockando. ■ Steep crow-stepped gables. In reasonable repair.

Lesmurdie. ▲ Octagonal with slated roof; weathervane gone.

Lethen. Behind the mansion (information from Commander R. M. Douglas).

Leuchars. ● Dated 1583. Collapsed.

Milton Brodie. ■ Dated 1769. Four dove holes in roof; ball ornaments on gables. Recently removed.

Milton Duff. ■ Originally stone slab roof; reroofed with slates in 1970.

New Elgin. ☉ Two stringcourses. In good order.

New Spynie. ■ Probably 15th century. Stone slab roof with square cupola; altered by addition of dormer on left of roof.

Orton House. ● Large with potence; entrance holes in wooden cupola.

Pitgavenny. ● Stone slab conical roof; entrance holes in south wall. In good repair.

Pittendreich. ■ Stone slab ridge-roof with ball finials; entrance holes in roof. In excellent order.

Urquhart Manse. ■ Built of boulders with clay and straw.

Wester Elchies. ■ One stringcourse.

A. Niven Robertson mentions four cotes that have disappeared in Morayshire.

NAIRNSHIRE

Boath House.* White-washed, with moulded cornice; conical slated roof; six dove holes above landing ledge with oblong window above. (N.T.S.) (Fig. 14).

Brackla House. ■■■ Small cote with dormer in roof of wood and felt.

Craggie. ● Slated cone roof above stringcourse; two sets of six entrance holes.

Kilravock Castle. T. Entrance by ladder; slated cone roof with square wooden cupola.

A. Niven Robertson listed five cotes which have gone in Nairnshire.

INVERNESS-SHIRE

Beaufort Castle – 'old stone doocot' mentioned by Lord Lovat in his book 'March Past'. Not found in 1980.

Belladrum House, Kiltarlity. ■■■ Ruinous; no roof; no nestholes.

Belladrum House. F. In clocktower at entrance to offices; four rows of blocked entrance holes.

Culloden House.* ▲ Octagonal with 8-sided pyramidal roof; remains of potence.

Foyers. Mid 18th century.

Inshes House. ■■■ Stone ridge-roof; two windows in south wall and one each on north and west walls; Bell-cote on top of north gable. Said to have been used by Prince Charles Edward Stuart. Gun-loops on lower floor.

Newton House, Kirkhill. ● Dated 1783. In good order, with remains of potence.

Urquhart Castle. ● Ruinous; only four nests remain.

A. Niven Robertson mentions two cotes that have disappeared in Inverness-shire.

Allangrange House. ■ Deteriorating with collapsed dormer window. Not found in 1980.

Braelangwell House. F. Square tower over farm offices archway; unusual dove holes in three large semicircular stones.

Cadboll. ■ Dated 1805. Typical lean-to cote with five ball finials; metal scarecrow on back wall.

Conon House.* ▲ Hexagonal; entrance holes in walls and in dormer window; occupied by crows.

Conon Mains.* F. Dated 1822. Mason work by Hugh Miller. Octagonal bell tower in farm court.

Cromarty House. F. In farm court; octagonal wooden cote. Not found in 1980.

Dingwall Castle. ▲ Battlemented octagonal tower called the 'Bishop's Dovecote'; slit windows; only 17 nest holes left.

Douglas Farm, Nigg. F. Over arch of farm offices.

Dunskeath House. ● Small one in bend of battlemented stone wall; no nest holes.

Geanies House. ■ Corrugated iron roof; weathervane; still used by doves.

Invergordon House. F. Dated 1810. Square tower over pend.

Kincraig House. F. Square tower in offices; peculiar entrance holes.

Mounteagle House. F. Over farm entrance.

Newhall House. F. Similar to Braelangwell, but more pigeon holes.

Ord Farm. F. Small one in farm buildings.

Pitcalzean House. F. Rectangular cote with ridge-roof.

Poyntzfield House. F. Offices destroyed by fire about 1975. Not found in 1980.

Raddery School. F. Over arch in farm court; entrance holes now occluded.

Tarradale House. F. Octagonal tower over farm court entrance; oval dove holes; cupola roof.

Tulloch Castle. F. Square tower over pend; entrance holes sealed.

A. Niven Robertson refers to six cotes which have vanished in Ross-shire.

SUTHERLAND

Dunrobin Castle. ■ Small square cote with pyramidal roof with dormer.

CAITHNESS

Ackergill Tower. ■■ ■■ Two 18th century.
Dale House, Halkirk. ⊙ 18th century. Three stringcourses; ruinous.
Dunbeath Castle. 18th century.
Forse House, Latheron.* ⊡ Two dormers each with four entrance holes; ball finials on back wall and stone thistle with weathervane.
Freswick House, Canisby. ⊙ Three stringcourses; stone nests.
Stemster House. ■ 18th century. Ridge-roof; dilapidated.
Stroma, *Isle of, Canisby. ■■ Dated 1677. In old graveyard; basement used as burial vault.

ARGYLL

Carlunan,* Inveraray. ● Slated conical roof with large louvre. In good order. Grass growing on roof.
Carskey. ▲ ▲ Two octagonal cotes.
Glen Barr, Kintyre. ■■

INNER AND OUTER ISLES

Benbecula, House of Clanranald. John Gladstone noted that a friend had shown him a photograph of one here, but gives no details. According to Mrs John Campbell of Canna, this vanished some years ago.
Iona Abbey. T. Nests in tower.
Rothesay Castle, Bute. T. Ruinous circular cote in castle; over two hundred nests visible.
Torosay Castle, Mull.* T. Battlemented tower; pyramidal slated roof; entrance holes below parapet.

ORKNEY

Balfour Castle.
Berstane, Kirkwall. ■■ 18th century with crests.
Cleat, Westray. F. In west gable of farm building.
Grainback, Kirkwall. ■■ Roofed with large stone slabs; entrance holes in gables.
Hall of Rendall.* ⊙ Dated 1648. Irregular nestholes. Collapsing.
Holland, Papa Westray. 17th century.
Lopness, Lady ■■ 18th century.
Melsetter, Longhope. 18th century.
Scar House, Westove. ■■
Skaill, Sandwick.* ■■ 18th century. In excellent condition; still used by pigeons.
Warsetter, Cross and Burness. Dated 1613.
Woodwick, Evie. ■■ 1648. Asymmetrical ridge-roof.

SHETLAND

Sand Lodge, Voe. ■ Square, brick; ogee pyramidal roof.

Addenda

EAST LOTHIAN   Page 32 33

Biel ⊓ West chamber slated roof; no roof on east one. Red sandstone. In west side remains of potence with ladder. Pigeons.

Pencaitland.* ■■ Roof now repaired. Iron hoops gone.

MIDLOTHIAN   Page 34

Ashley House. F. Victorian with ridge roof, finials and six entrance holes.

LANARKSHIRE   Page 39

Cartland Bridge Hotel, Lanark. F. two triangular dormer windows, each with three entrance holes. No nestholes.